WHAT TO DO WHEN JANE KNOWS DICK ABOUT DATING

IF HE WANTS YOU, YOU WILL KNOW IT

LAURA J. WELLINGTON

Post Hill
PRESS

A POST HILL PRESS BOOK
ISBN: 978-1-68261-530-0
ISBN (eBook): 978-1-68261-531-7

What to Do When Jane Knows DICK About Dating:
If He Wants You, You Will Know It

Post Hill Press
New York • Nashville
posthillpress.com

Published in the United States of America

*To the two ladies I met in a pub in
Amsterdam who inspired this book.
And to my father, who gave me all
I needed to write it.*

TABLE OF CONTENTS

FOREWORD

Life. It has a way of catching you off guard and delivering you clarity all at the same time. In other words, after 16 years of marriage, I've now found myself thrust back into the dating scene. Before I could even begin the process, though, I had to take a long, hard look at what happened to my marriage and what, if any, role I had played in its slow spiral of death. Sometimes, we are too consumed with emotion to reflect and be honest about the choices we've made that put us in our current dilemma, but unless we alter our behavior, we are doomed to repeat it. I met my husband when I was 19 years old—old enough to vote, old enough to drive, but not wise enough to make the best choices for myself and certainly not for a healthy relationship.

Having been somewhat of an odd child growing up, I think my parents felt fortunate that I had found someone, anyone, who had a good head on his shoulders and worked hard. A draft horse, by comparison, can offer these same qualities. My parents were not picky and provided little guidance with regards to how I should find someone who was a good match for me.

With no solid dating experience, lacking any sound relationship advice, and reeking of teenage desperation, I floundered when trying to meet someone in my early years. I do not regret marrying the man I eventually did as I have three beautiful children now. I am also better prepared to make a wiser and more careful decision the next time (if there is one).

I met Laura Wellington a few years ago. Since then I've learned that her simple advice and no-nonsense approach to dating (and life) is something we could all use a little more of. This book will be a treat for you by bringing humor to what can be a stressful and frustrating experience. Whether new to dating or getting ready to jump off the merry-go-round, you may find these basic concepts helpful in building a healthy and sustainable relationship.

If the shoe doesn't fit, stop wasting your time trying to shoehorn it in.

Nicole Belanger
Writer, dater, and mom

INTRODUCTION

The idea for this book arose while I was taking a weeklong vacation in Amsterdam by myself. No... no one can accuse me of not being a confident, strong, and freewheeling woman. I don't wait for life to show up on my doorstep. I grab it—meeting each day with grace and gusto. Example: Amsterdam.

I needed a break, made sure that all of my ducks were in a row, and took off, trading in the lingering cold of the Connecticut shoreline for canals, bikes, tulips, and fries with mayonnaise (a favorite of mine). It was a perfect choice—exactly what I needed to rejuvenate my worn-out body and mind. I read, wrote, took in the sights, and acquainted myself with a ton of unfamiliar faces who soon became friends—two of whom, unexpectedly, inspired the writing of this book.

I met these ladies while sitting at a small table in a quaint pub. The pub was located within steps of my hotel, and I felt the need to venture out that evening as opposed to eating at one of the hotel's swanky restaurants or within the confines of my own room. As a "people person," I wanted to be among the natives as much as possible. So I walked down the street and made my way inside the pub.

Upon my entering, the bartender greeted me, then motioned for me to take a seat anywhere, so I did, one quite close to the bar. Hungry and struggling with the discomfort that arises from leaping across time zones, I quickly ordered, then opened up my NOOK and began to read while sipping a glass of chilled Sauvignon Blanc.

Page after page I turned, trying hard to concentrate. But my efforts could not match the interesting conversation taking place between two young women sitting at the bar. Before long, I became fully distracted.

The topic at hand was the very popular and confusing practice of dating. One woman was advising the other on what to do following a recent date that had, obviously, gone very wrong. The disappointment that ensued had ignited a fury of questions, the magnitude of which surely rivaled that required to finally achieve world peace. And I couldn't help but chuckle to myself as I marveled at how ridiculously complicated and muddled dating had become for these women and, frankly, for all single women.

Once a natural dance engaged in between men and women, today's dating seems anything but. The reasons for this are many, some *legitimate* while others **not particularly**, including the one that fosters the misconception that females and males are exactly the same and, thus, should approach dating in copycat form. Nothing could be further from the truth.

Such myths wreak havoc on the psyche of young, impressionable women eager to date but unsure of themselves and how to really go about it. All this, despite the independent image so many of them portray. *Egad!* Who would have thought that today's Jane would stumble so clumsily in front of Dick?

Needless to say, after enough time went by overhearing these two young women chatter back and forth about whether or not the suitor in question would make a proper second date based upon the failure of the first, I couldn't help but interrupt the conversation and their faulty train of thinking. After all, as I was already ushering three daughters of my own through the process of dating, the idea of leaving these two to ponder a question whose answer was so obvious...well, I just couldn't do it. I needed to help.

My welcomed input inspired an exchange that lasted for about an hour. At the end of it, there was no question in the young lady's mind that she should not continue to date this cad and both women suggested that I write a book—a reliable dating handbook to keep Jane on her feet and happily skipping towards Dick. After some thought, I agreed, and here you have it in your hot little hands.

Now you may ask, why the title, *What to Do When Jane Knows* **DICK** *About Dating: If He Wants You, You Will Know It*. The second half of it stems from a lesson my father taught me when I was ready to date. He said, "If you want to find out if a guy truly wants you, do nothing and watch what he does. Men who want you will make it obvious. Men who don't will make that obvious too."

So simple. So accurate. And yet so difficult for women to accept and follow, especially today's women, who thrive on immediate answers and constant motion. Patience is not exactly a virtue for many of them, nor is removing the guesswork from the equation. Reality speaks, however, that you needn't be a sleuth to figure out whether or not a man likes you. You just need to sit tight and keep your eyes peeled. His actions will say it all. They are the great clarifier for single women everywhere, I assure you.

Now what about the first half of the title—an obvious play on words arising from one of the most widely read elementary school book series, Dick and Jane? As that series helped many of us master one of the most basic required skills of all time, I figured it could help us master another by providing a fun way to write and frame this book. Look, the last thing you need is another dull, depressing dating book to pull from the shelf. I wanted to create a page-turner as unique as the woman who is reading it. Hopefully, I have done this. I'm sure I will find out.

Lastly, as the topic of dating is extremely vast, I decided to limit the focus of this particular book to the "meet and greet" portion of dating, comprised of the initial encounter followed by the first three months. Once two individuals move past this point, coupledom begins—a whole other animal and book to consider. For now, let's concentrate on tying those patent leathers onto your feet, tightly, and clearing your head of all of the nonsense that has kept you unhappily single and stuck in the dating pool for much longer than you ever expected. Might I also suggest that you stop listening to any counterproductive dating advice from those who don't know Dick and will, ultimately, prevent you from meeting him too? You deserve more, and this book will help you get it.

The bell is ringing, Jane. Time to go back to school and relearn the ABCs of dating.

<u>Reality</u>
Dick and Jane are not the same;
And if they were,
They'd have one brain.

CHAPTER 1

DICK AND JANE ARE NOT THE SAME

Whoever convinced women that they are the same as men is a genius (and I say this sarcastically). Men and women are not the *same* and never will be so long as sex exists between us. It may be inconvenient and unacceptable to some for ideological reasons, but that does not make it any less true. Men and women are different, from our unique anatomies up through how we use our brains. Our hardwiring is undeniably distinct, which will continue to stymie all claims of absolute sameness as well as dramatically impact the manner in which both sexes approach dating.

For most women, dating is a means to an end, that end being marriage and children. For men, this may not be so. There are many Dicks out there who are simply looking for a good time, which interpreted means as many Janes in their beds as physically possible on the way to their particular "end." College campuses, local bars, and dating websites are full of them, as are airports, shopping malls, work environments, and just about everywhere else Jane roams.

None of this behavior is new, mind you, except for the fact that it seems more open and widely tolerated than ever before. Additionally, certain Janes feel the need to mimic Dick's unruly behavior—proof to the rest of the world of just how grown-up and closely similar to the opposite sex they are. Those women who don't play along basically get tossed from the sandbox—which is not nice and quite deserving of a trip to the principal's office and a cautionary note home to the parents if you ask me.

There is no doubt that we women have complete control over whom we share our cookies with, but to correlate the blatant satisfaction of basic primal urges with that of some newfound awakening among women is rather daft. Jane may play with dogs but she shouldn't strive to become one or lie down with all of them. Nor should she adopt a one-size-fits-all policy when none of what's included fits her persona or overall life. All women have the right to choose what's right for them, without judgment or backlash from those who think otherwise. Whatever that decision, however, it will not bring our gender even remotely closer to being the same as men.

It will also in no way ensure our equality; in fact, it will detract from it—as, in needing to be the *same* as our sexual counterparts, we are basically admitting that we are lesser in our current form. I don't consider myself *lesser*. Do you? And surely Mother Nature doesn't, given the monumental role she has charged women with playing in perpetuating the species. If we should learn anything from the Dicks who keep bouncing their balls in the air, it should be the value of not doing so, individually and as a whole.

That said, let me reassure you. There are many incredible Dicks gathered in the schoolyard who are eager and happy to play catch with one Jane. Just don't expect their preference for monogamy to mean that they are just like you, especially when it comes to communicating their initial attraction or ultimate desire to date you. When it comes to both scenarios, men have only two crayons in their coloring box—black and white—while women enjoy a sweeping array of shades.

It is this difference that makes it difficult for women to recognize, interpret, and accept the cues from men regarding their romantic interest in them. And yet, nothing good comes from our need to color the black-and-white pictures drawn out for us by them. Men are very literal and intentional beings, and so is the manner in which they communicate. In other words, if you have to guess at whether or not a man wants you, he doesn't—and adding color to his picture won't change that. It will just prolong the disappointment for you. Better you simply accept reality and move you and your crayons over to the next available desk.

Now, some would make the case that you could change his mind if the opportunity arises to do so, and yes, there are exceptions to every rule. But ask yourself this: "Do I really have the time to waste trying? Is he truly so outstanding that I am willing to forgo the man who trips over his own two feet the minute he lays eyes on me?" My answer would be no.

It's disheartening to see how easily so many Janes trade away their own specialness for snip-pets of attention from men who barely even know they are alive. Watching moments like this unfold is as painful to me as nails on a chalkboard, especially knowing that there is no logic or evidence to support this type of thinking—quite the contrary. Although the factors that make a woman attractive from one man to another vary, there are undoubtedly a few absolutes all men can agree upon—one being the confidence a woman projects as a result of understanding her own self-worth. This characteristic is intoxicating to men and should be equally as valued by you. To strive for anything less than an A-plus here is to all but guarantee a tough dating road ahead, I assure you.

What Jane always has to remember when encountering each new Dick is that her attractiveness, lovability, and specialness do not rise or fall based upon whether or not his genitalia does. Chemistry is fickle by nature, and so is every one of us. The fact that personal preferences may not align doesn't mean your pigtail isn't worth pulling. It simply means that you've missed out on an unnecessary headache.

If, however, Dick suddenly begins to stare all googly-eyed at you or plops himself next to you at circle time, rest assured, he's itchin' for a kiss. Same thing holds true if he takes the bar stool beside you and strikes up a conversation. In both cases, he's made his interest known. Now it is up to you to decide if a game of show-and-tell is in the cards...in other words, "Is this Dick worth getting to know?"

An answer of no almost always means a kind but firm rejection. But an answer of yes? That type of excitement can carry you for days. Revel in it, find the perfect party dress, and relish the attention. It's a one-in-a-million feeling—enviable by anyone who has ever been in love or wants to be. And today, you are that one.

CHAPTER 2

JANE DOES "NOTHING" WELL

We all know her...the Jane in the classroom who has all the boys buzzing. The popular girl whose unwavering self-esteem places her center stage and makes her unconcerned with others' approval. She's not always the most beautiful, most intelligent, or most friendly. To some, she may even seem removed and rather off-putting, but to Dicks everywhere, she is the Jane of their dreams merely because this Jane ain't about to acquiesce to no boy!

She comes first in her head, which includes her hobbies, friends, studies, sports, and just about anything else she fancies. Focusing on herself has made her fascinating, self-assured, and somewhat inaccessible. It's also made her a challenge to men, and if you haven't learned already...all men like a challenge. Their competitive nature thrives on it.

When a woman is comfortable in her own skin, dating becomes easier for her, because she isn't relying on meeting the right Dick to make her happy. She's built her life on a solid platform, according to her own standards.

Men love this type of woman because she projects an air of self-sufficiency and confidence, none of which arose at the hands of a man. She literally needs to do nothing to attract him and makes for a very interesting date and highly coveted catch.

This Jane's biggest issue is *who* to choose. How to handle him when she figures this out is easy. She's going to make him pull the little red wagon for a while—because she can and because she knows that it is the best way to reveal to her who this Dick truly is.

The worst thing a woman can do is make it too easy for a man during the initial stage of dating. Men tend to move aggressively when really interested in women. There are many women who will allow themselves to be overwhelmed by this, resulting in short-lived romantic encounters. Janes who are confident and dating-savvy will meet this behavior with pushback, making them even more appealing to these Dicks. This does not mean that they will adopt a temperament likened to that of a she-devil. It just means that they won't lie down easily, metaphorically or literally.

The more a woman makes a man jump rope, the better, as it will allow her to set the tone, gauge expectations, and establish respect between the two. For him, knowing that she is not a pushover will either up his attraction for her or send him fleeing. Either way, she wins, which includes deciding what the next step should be.

That said, obstacle courses can be run for only so long. Eventually, a man needs to know that there is an end in sight and at that end is a woman who wants to become his best friend and biggest cheerleader. After all, isn't that what dating is truly all about? Two kids equally determined to figure out if they are aptly suited for an eternal playdate together? Absolutely.

For many men, the key to figuring this out revolves around two words—"time" and "attention." Consider your Dick like that bean plant your second grade teacher forced you to grow. In order for it to have flourished, you had to make sure that you devoted *time* and *attention* to caring for it; otherwise, no beans. The same holds true for boyfriends.

If your goal is to launch a successful dating relationship with your chosen Dick, you need to eventually expand your priorities from just *you* to 'him and you.' Keep in mind, this revelation in no way translates to your taking a back seat to him on the classroom seating chart. It means that you sit beside him (or in front of him in certain cases) and flash him a proud smile every time he answers a question correctly.

Men need this type of confirmation and support from the women they are dating. It makes them feel invincible and powerful (like a superhero) in the eyes of the most important people in the world to them.

No doubt, this dynamic stems from the mother-son relationship, but regardless, we inherit those boys and so too do we inherit the superhero storyline, whether or not we like the idea of having to perpetuate it.

I can tell you that if you do perpetuate it, you will reap many rewards along the way, including having your own personal superhero around to save the day every time it feels like it is heading south. Some Dicks make truly awesome superheroes, and there is something to be said for learning what special powers yours has to change a sucky moment into one that brings you both closer.

CHAPTER 3

JANE DOES "EVERYTHING" POORLY

She's probably familiar to you—the Jane who does "everything" poorly. Most of us have been her at one time or another. Many of us, during the early stages of discovering boys. That's pretty understandable, as anything new is usually done poorly and learning how to interact with boys is no exception.

What is painful, however, is to observe women, who fail to grow up and out of this awkward stage, struggle to date. These episodes are terrifying to witness because these women seem to be the only ones unclear about what is truly happening.

This Jane doesn't seem to take cues well. Instead of realizing the discomfort being caused by her flirtation with a disinterested Dick, she continues it and even doubles down. The more he resists, the more she tries to draw him out, despite the fact that both he and she are slowly succumbing to asphyxiation by all the desperation flooding the room.

Frankly put, this Jane has placed herself in the position of being unattractive to any worthwhile Dick who comes along, and two reasons are at the core. First, she knows not how to play the game, and second, she's needy. Neither screams "hot mama" nor bodes well for her dating future.

This Jane should take a step back and re-evaluate her success record when it comes to attracting the attention of a man. She needs to grasp the value that she brings to the table and hold on tight. And she needs to realize that all potential for romance is facing destruction at the hands of her own insecurities. Then she needs to *Stop It*!

I can't emphasize this enough. If she doesn't do so, she might as well walk herself over to the local animal rescue center and adopt a cat. She would be better off, especially as cats have nine lives unlike men. Her odds are higher that the cat will stick around longer.

CHAPTER 4

DICK PULLS THE LITTLE RED WAGON

What should you expect from Dick when you pass the handle of the little red wagon his way?

Everything and anything. The answer is all up to you. You simply need to make your expectations known (and do so clearly), then sit back and wait to see if this man will meet them. I caution you, however, to make sure that what you say you want, you truly do want, because when he brings it to you, your response needs to be a pleased one. Don't ask for a puppy, then wish he'd wheeled in a kitten. That won't do.

Men need to feel that they have done a good job and changing your expectations midstream won't help them achieve this. They need to know that if they meet your desires, you will recognize them for the stellar providers and superheroes they are. Flash them a great big smile, wrap your arms around them, and tell them that they are wonderful. They will be back out to get that kitten in no time (so that the puppy has a friend).

It's also important that you watch to see if, by the end of three months of dating, they begin to slack on pulling that red wagon around or leave it on the driveway amid a downpour while they go running off to join their friends to jump in mud puddles. That's an important sign, because it means that you are either becoming less of a concern for him or he is becoming increasingly comfortable with you, whereby you need to decide if his behavior is acceptable. Keep in mind, if you decide it isn't and say nothing, don't cry in your milk when he drops the ball in other areas of your dating life as well. And he will, which brings me to a vital point that most women fail to realize and react to until they are a few Dicks in.

Succinctly put, if a man is doing something that doesn't work for you, it doesn't work...period! This remains true even if everyone else in the world disagrees with you. It doesn't matter. You need to respect yourself enough to react to his behavior in a way that will work out best for the two of you. Women have the tendency to overlook situations that feel wrong to them, only to regret doing so somewhere down the line.

Most Dicks would much rather you tell them what's irking you than have you hold it in and against them. Giving them a chance to correct whatever it is, explain it, or refuse to do anything about it is much better than not. It represents another aspect of his desire to pull the little red wagon.

Additionally, giving Dick the opportunity to show off to you of his own volition is extremely important. You won't know what a man *can* or *will* do to romance you or keep you entertained until you let him and his little red wagon loose. This is the fun part of having a wagon between you. It opens your dating door to memorable surprises and a great deal of learning, which can carry the both of you for three months, three years or more than three decades.

I speak from experience, as the wonderful young man I chose to date in my 20s was the same wonderful middle-aged man who struggled to his feet and toasted me at the surprise birthday party he arranged and hosted in my honor just days prior to his passing away from cancer. If you question whether or not I know what I am talking about, question no more. I get it and am trying to prevent you from wasting time *getting it* too.

Give your Dick the space to pull his little red wagon around anywhere he wants to go as much as he needs to. You just hop in and enjoy the ride. I promise you, you will be happy you did. It's some of the best *play* you will ever experience in your life.

CHAPTER 5

DICK PICKS JANE FLOWERS

When Dick shows up at your doorstep with a bouquet of freshly picked dandelions, welcome him into the kitchen and thank him for what seems to be the most beautiful bouquet of flowers you have ever received. The fact is, if you really like him, it will be. If you don't, it won't. It is as simple as that and yet, for some Janes, not so much.

I marvel at how many women fail to acknowledge or accept their discontent with a man just because they prefer not be alone. They'd rather spend time trying to fit a square peg in a round hole than call it quits. I don't get this kind of logic and I don't respect it.

If you really don't like a guy, have the human decency to be honest with him. If love isn't in the cards, *respect* makes a great second place. This Dick might even know another Dick who will, in fact, be the perfect match for you. Give him a good reason to make the introduction by being a Jane of character. You will like yourself a whole lot better for it.

Now let's say that dandelions have always been one of your least favorite flowers or that you are actually allergic to them. Both scenarios call for different styles of responses to prevent any repeats down the line. The former requires indirect communication, and the latter, direct. Let's take the latter first, as it is the easiest and most critical.

If your special Dick has unknowingly placed you in harm's way, simply tell him as nicely as possible while keeping your distance for the obvious reasons. This is information he needs to know and telling him will ignite his desire to protect you. Expect him to about-face and march himself back outside to toss those buds to the bottom of the trash can in superhero-like form.

If, however, dandelions are just not your cup of tea and you really love tiger lilies instead, say nothing at this particular juncture. In fact, find the most beautiful of all vases, fill it with water, and carefully place the dandelions inside while praising your Dick for his thoughtfulness. Then bring them upstairs and place them at the side of your bed, realizing that the true significance in this moment is that the man you care for did a really nice thing for you and that means more than the actual flowers themselves.

Your Dick will appreciate your reaction, and you will set the tone for future thoughtful gestures of all kinds—one of which will probably be a vase filled with tiger lilies, given you eventually share with him that you have always loved them too. I urge you, though, not to reveal this new information while still lingering in the aftereffects of those dandelions. Timing is everything, and it's no different when communicating with your man.

Now, some women will scream at the idea that you didn't just tell him your true feelings altogether, stating that your Dick should be able to handle it and move on. "Why put yourself through so much work?" is what they will argue, followed by, "Seems dishonest." My answer would be to direct them back to Chapter 1 for a quick review.

There is no doubt that it would be so much simpler if we Janes did not have to handle our Dicks with kid gloves at times, but the fact of the matter is, we do. Certain situations just resolve themselves more quickly and easily if we learn the art of *indirect* communication. And, frankly, the more you practice, the better you become at it. For instance, if your Dick has the fashion sense of a clown, make a present of some great-looking shirts and break him out of the circus. Showing him what you like in clothing will inspire him to wear it and even buy it for himself in the future. He will also really appreciate that you bought him a gift, as men like presents too and for the very same reasons we Janes do.

The worst thing you can do in this instance (and any instance) is to criticize him, as men never take criticism well, especially from the women they are trying to impress. It's hurtful to them and goes against everything "superhero" in their heads.

It is much better to add a few extra steps into the mix so that the result you want is exactly what you get. And if you don't know it yet, smart Dicks do the same thing to us too—although they term the practice "survival."

CHAPTER 6

DICK NEEDS A SPANKIN'

Let me begin by stating that I don't condone the spanking of kids, adults, or animals of any kind... *ever*! I do, however, understand what it feels like when Dick makes a mistake or worse yet, does something really wrong. You sometimes just want to smack him... but you don't.

What I have learned is that, in most of these instances and especially during the early months of dating, giving your Dick the *benefit of the doubt* when he suddenly disappoints is better than not. Many times, he truly has no idea what he did to upset you and would take it all back in a heartbeat if he could.

We Janes sometimes forget, however, what it is that is driving the little red wagon. We also have a tendency during such moments to get stuck in our own heads, cornered by demented narratives left over from past relationships. Without any real justification, we react to our Dicks as if hideous crimes have been purposely committed, leading to one of three outcomes: our first real argument, our last real argument or the need for us to apologize even more than him. The turning of the table is dumbfounding for many of us, to say the least.

It is for this reason that I, again, *normally* recommend you give your man the benefit of the doubt when a blunder has been made or when you dislike a particular behavior he is exhibiting. It just could be that Dick knows not what he does, and so you must tell him without shanking him as you are doing so.

For example, if your Dick's teasing sometimes crosses the line—leaving you feeling embarrassed and even demeaned—tell him how you feel in a calm, nonjudgmental way so that he may actually hear you and correct his behavior. Sometimes guys don't realize how coarse and offensive their humor can be because they are so used to joking around with other guys. It's an innocent mistake, and one that can easily be corrected. He'll probably be quite happy that you did. If, however, he is not, better you know that early so that you can decide if this kind of behavior is something you are willing to live with or need to erase from your life with one of those big, fat, jumbo-sized erasers that you still can't believe exist. Old habits die hard and, apparently, this one is sticking around for a while or possibly forever.

Keep in mind, your decision to assume the best of him during moments of question or grave concern should not prevent you from continuing to use your brain. If 1 + 1 = 2 but your Dick keeps coming up with reasons why 1 + 1 actually = 3, you may just have to give him a detention for thinking that you are such a dunce, then consider whether or not you want to continue walking home with him. He's showing you the best of what he's got in the dawn of your dating life together, and if what he's got adds up to him being a liar, call a recess and take your marbles home.

There are plenty of Dicks looking for intelligent women to date, I assure you. Be thankful that yours revealed himself when he did and go find another more worthy of your time.

Surprise

I met Dick;
My heart did tick.
He met me;
His heart did flee.
It was the quickest date in history.

CHAPTER 7

JANE AND THE THREE DICKS

You would think I was talking about the butcher, the baker, and the candlestick maker, but I am not, although they share some similarities—none of which are good, I must say. The men I am speaking of are the loner, the joker, and the guy whose umbilical cord is securely fastened to his buddies. I recommend avoiding each one of them, as they don't make great dates or relationship material. This doesn't mean that they are not sexy, entertaining to listen to, or even uniquely interesting. It means that their downsides usually outweigh their upsides and many times will land you on your backside bawling about them on the bed.

Let's take the loner to begin with. This guy is alone for a reason. He prefers it. And try as you might to integrate him into your life, your friend group, and maybe even your family, ultimately, he will not make it a joyful endeavor. Nor will he ever feel comfortable. Odds are, you will unknowingly slip into his world before he conquers yours to any real extent, until one day you wake up and realize that his is the only face you have seen for a while.

Loners also tend to be fairly negative people, and their influence can come out in you in ways that leave you barely recognizing yourself. Many women who date loners begin to experience an increase in negative thinking themselves. Others become depressed. Still others become resentful of the isolation loners mire them in. Eventually, they break free of the dating routine altogether. Once this happens, many Janes can't believe how they ever got involved with a loner in the first place. The answer is quite simple: The loner seems mysterious, and lots of women are eager to solve the mystery.

Let me save you some time. The loner isn't mysterious. He just wants to be left alone. Do yourself a favor and accommodate him, as there is nothing to be gained by not. One last thing: Many loners have issues that are out of the ordinary, including feeling victimized by just about everyone and everything. Unless you have a deep-seated desire to play full-time therapist to him, back away and look for a more stable Dick to hold on to.

Now, let's talk about the joker. When I say "joker" in this case, I'm not referring to the guy who can keep you in stitches. I am talking about the sarcastic guy who makes his jokes at your expense—the one who ridicules you, then follows up his bad taste with a "haha." When you don't agree with his humor, he will make you feel as if you can't take a joke, adding insult to injury. This Dick is his own best audience. He is insensitive, obnoxious, and emotionally abusive. And he is a repeat offender (not the guy who has the occasional misstep). Dump that Dick as quickly as you can before he beats you into putty.

The last Dick you have to concern yourself with is the guy who comes in a six-pack—him and five buddies. This is the man who is most apt to make you his trophy girlfriend, then shelve you regularly so that he can go everywhere his pals are headed. Some of his favorite hangouts are sporting events, bars, and Las Vegas. This isn't the man who once in a while meets up with his friends and goes for a beer. He's the Dick who once in a while meets up with you, and when he does, he's nearly forgotten your name.

Sign onto the notion that you will always take a backseat to his buddies, then sign off of him. Even if you think you can deal with his absenteeism now, it will eventually grow old and so will *you* to him, especially if you begin nagging him to change. Save both of you the distress and send him back to the arms of those he truly loves. Either that or find yourself a very detailed hobby or group of Janes readily available to occupy your time when he isn't. It's not how I would choose to have a dating relationship.

Let me just emphasize that with each of these situations and men, there are exceptions. But as a gener-

41

al rule of thumb—and knowing that my evaluation of these Dicks is pretty spot-on—I recommend you earnestly avoid dating them. They are more hassle than they are worth. They will also take time away from your meeting anyone else. Why do that to yourself when you deserve so much more.

CHAPTER 8

DICK HAS WARTS. GROSS!

No matter how you slice it, even the best Dicks have warts. The warts may not be so readily apparent upon meeting or during the first three months thereafter. But he's got 'em, and they will show up eventually. When they do, you are going to have to decide if you can live with them. Surprisingly, some of the most annoying warts catch you off-guard, as they arise from a characteristic about your Dick that you initially loved. You would think this would not be the case, but many a Jane will testify that it undoubtedly is—me included.

When I was dating my late husband, I thought it was absolutely adorable that he loved to play guitar and sing, despite the fact that he was completely tone-deaf and had no real musical talent whatsoever. His determination to overcome these deficiencies, however, somehow endeared him to me, and I'd listen to him for hours croon and strum his heart out.

Fast-forward five years. I could barely hold my request for silence whenever I saw him pick up the guitar. I did hold it, mind you, because it was more important to me to save his feelings than hear him play, but it took all of my fortitude and patience to cope with the screeching that would ensue. I look back now and laugh, but it's true.

It's a wart I invited onto myself in deciding to marry the man. And I lived with it, acceptingly, because I wanted to live with him. For me, though, there are some warts that are just too large and ugly to overlook, *cheating* being one of them.

I stand firm in my conviction that "once a cheater, always a cheater." A Dick who has gotten away with pulling the wool over another Jane's eyes in the past will certainly try the same with you. And no, you are not *different*, even when he adamantly insists that you are and that he's telling the truth. Give it enough time and you will find out otherwise, I assure you.

Cheating is a wart that I could never live with, mainly because it violates the "trust" and "mutual respect" I require. Other women can (and will) cope with it for reasons that span everything from cultural conditioning to fear to the ability to separate *feelings* from the act itself. I'm not quite sure how this changes the significance of this type of infraction at all, but it does for them.

In my opinion, a good-looking Dick can become mighty ugly fast if he's discovered in the coat closet with the wrong Jane. And an ugly Dick can become pretty damn attractive if he keeps his namesake in check no matter how many Janes throw themselves his way. I'd take the latter over the former any day, and so would countless other women who learned that lesson the hard way. It's a wart that leaves a scar, for sure.

The good thing about warts is, if you decide to live with them, they actually can bring the dating couple closer. After all, neither Dick nor Jane shows his or her warts to just anybody. It takes a certain amount of trust between the two of you to share such vulnerabilities. By revealing what is sacred to each other, you grow together and so does your affection for each other and your dependency upon each other.

Ultimately, discovering and learning to accept (or not) your Dick's warts is a very good thing. Just remember, when in doubt, give it time. You will soon find out if a particular wart becomes yet another feather in your joint dating cap or one that makes your skin crawl.

CHAPTER 9

DICK SHOVES JANE HARD

No, I don't mean in the physical sense of the word, although we will address this issue down the line. What I am referring to here is the Dick who can't seem to push the relationship forward fast enough for his taste. Every Jane meets him once in a while, and it feels almost baffling when you do.

We've become so used to Dicks who delay relationship progress that we are wary of the unexpected few who actually want to run with the ball—the ones who will meet you at the park on time (or even a bit early) with an extra bottle of water in hand (for you) and maybe even a plan already tucked up his sleeve for the next time the two of you get together. And although our initial reaction to this Dick's consideration and enthusiasm about dating us is being undeniably thrilled, many Janes may also respond with alarm or even begin to feel repulsed—quite an odd way to react towards a man who merely refuses to play games, and yet it happens all the time.

Have our dating lives become so devoid of thoughtful gestures and excitement or has our self-worth as women become so diminished by the dating scene that we can't even recognize a great guy when we see him or know what healthy dating actually looks like? I'd say for many, the answer is yes. We don't want the games, but we also don't know what to do when a guy has tossed out the board and all his broken pieces.

Time to wake up, ladies! These Dicks do exist and can be enormously fun to date, especially because they are eager to proactively participate in the dating process. Many are wildly romantic as well, which is a nice revelation and a bonus to realize. It's a short term benefit that pays off big in the long term as well, I assure you.

This Dick is not the Dick to run away from but the Dick to run with. The worst that can happen is that you may need to rein him in a bit as you do.

I will admit, however, that there are some Dicks who exhibit similar behavior who are rushing you along solely because they actually have something to hide. Don't be flattered by this Dick's impatience; be frightened, as this man's need to rush you probably arises from reasons you would be much better living without, including everything from low self-esteem to self-loathing and more.

This Dick is the one you do have to exert caution with. Listen to the alarm sounding in your head and make sure you date him slowly. Time is your best friend always, but especially in this particular case. If he can't accept your decision to adopt a pace you are comfortable with, stop dating him, as his sense of urgency is trumping your need for respect. That's the mother of all red flags and indicates some very real problems both now and ahead.

CHAPTER 10

DICK IS DAMN GOOD-LOOKING

The last of the Dicks that I am going to focus on is the Dick who sweeps you off your feet through good looks alone. Some of these Dicks are inarguably wonderful men, while others are true assholes. Either way, all of them have been blessed with pretty faces, placing them immediately at the head of the class when it comes to most Janes.

Whereas these Dicks hardly have to work at all to wrangle a date, average-looking Dicks normally have to work twice as hard, and even then, most young and inexperienced Janes will choose the former over the latter every time. And why not? It's fun to hang on to the Dick every Jane wants to call her own.

As time goes by, however, this Dick may lose his luster, his increasingly familiar face now less enthralling. It happens more than you expect. Ever wonder where the old phrase "Familiarity breeds contempt" comes from? The answer is, all of the women who married men they originally insisted they'd never tire of gazing at...then they did. Looks fade due to age, anger, and absence. It is for this reason that you need to judge your Dick on more than just his beautiful head and why you should weigh the merits of average-looking Dicks too.

The beauty of going out with an average-looking man is that he knows he has to differentiate himself from the pack through initiative rather than relying on physical appearance. Therefore, he can make for a very interesting and creative date who is used to working hard too. This bodes well for your future, something women with marital ambitions need to keep in mind, even during the first three months of dating.

Ultimately, whichever Dick you choose, you must do so understanding that if your dating life leaves a lot to be desired today, it will be that much worse tomorrow. What you see now is what you are going to live with or die from later. So choose your Dick realizing that this is the best you're gonna get, and if what he has to offer is just not satisfying you, let him go and find another.

50

CHAPTER 11

JANE OPENS THE DOOR

Never pursue a man! You heard me. This statement may seem outlandish by today's standards, but it is true. Why? Because times may have changed, but the core of men truly hasn't.

Men are still hunters. The fact that modern-day society has removed much of their opportunity to actually hunt makes it even more important to allow them to do so here. The chase is still part of the fun for them, and so it is for most women too. Don't remove it from the equation. Open the door to it and see what Dick can do.

Drop your pencil in front of him and see how quickly he scoops it up. Walk his way to class and notice if he looks up and flashes a smile. Corny? Yes, but also effective. Women for years have been thinking up non-obvious ways to create the "opening" for men, and they have been doing so because they are intelligent enough to realize that both Dick and Jane get what they want and need by remaining true to form. Men become empowered and excited by the chase, and women do, too, but in a markedly different way.

By Dick pursuing Jane, he is revealing that she exerts enormous power over him, setting the tone for a healthy, respect-filled, and satisfying dating relationship for the two of them. If, however, Jane sets out to pursue Dick, Dick knows—right off the bat—that he holds all the cards. Not good, I assure you, as you are basically confirming in both Dick's heads that you are neither valuable nor special enough to coax his pursuit or any other Dick's for that matter. How is that attractive? It isn't.

Even if he decides to fight his natural proclivities and give this dating thing a shot with you, under these new and unfamiliar circumstances, the odds that dating each other will ever feel truly comfortable are extremely low. Don't be surprised if you become an afterthought for him rather quickly.

Alternately, if he somehow decides to hang in there for a while and ultimately realizes that he really does like you, the trade-off you initially made might just come back to haunt you. Because he no longer feels the need to pursue you for anything, you may just find that you now need to pursue him for everything, eventually provoking you to ask the question, "What's in this for me?" Good question. That answer is, most likely, nothing.

It is much better to play the game as Mother Nature intended it to be played. That grande dame has been around for years, and she's not about to lose easily to a mere mortal. Learn the rules. Wait your turn. And stop negating reality!

CHAPTER 12

JANE TREADS CAREFULLY

Even the toughest Dicks can fall hard, and a woman can actually see it when it happens. There is a noticeable shift in Dick's demeanor when he is around you. He transitions from liking you to more. Then, finally, he switches gears again, committing his heart fully. You can see the transformation in his face and in his behavior. He loves you, and he can hardly contain the news.

If you have ever seen this progression in your Dick, you know what I mean. It's wonderful to watch and definitely freeing for the two of you. Straps off, you can now explore your relationship on a deeper level, without concern that one of you will be running away anytime soon.

But what happens to this man if, after he takes the plunge, the relationship doesn't work out? It goes sour, breaking his heart and messing up his head. The answer is, he looks for another Jane to appease him, to help him heal, and to make him feel lovable and important again. Is it any wonder the phrase "The best way to get over someone is to get under someone" has become so popular on college campuses today? I think the answer is obvious. Women do it too, mind you, but less.

Rebounding in the arms of another woman is a classic fix for men who have found themselves in the devastating position of being suddenly kicked to the curb. It's their foolproof way of making themselves feel better, helping place them back on their feet and moving forward again. For the women in their paths, however, a ton of pain may ensue if they take the chance of becoming the next woman and then potentially the *transitional* one—the bridge between two significant relationships with neither including her. I recommend that you try not to fall into this trap or you might very well find yourself in the exact same position tomorrow that you are helping him through today.

All that being said, there are cases when the woman Dick chooses to rebound with actually becomes his next long relationship due to the indestructible bond that arose from the comfort she brought to him through this very difficult time in his life. In helping him heal, she provided a safe haven for him to lick his wounds, learn about her, and establish a foundation of trust, respect, gratitude, and more—key elements in the building of a healthy relationship. Once fully over the other woman, Dick may look back on his heartbreak as the best thing that ever happened to him because it opened the door to a stronger relationship and newfound happiness.

Still, any woman who accepts the risk of becoming the rebound Jane needs to go into this situation with her eyes wide open and tread cautiously. Conversely, if Jane is the one emerging from a bad breakup, she must consider the possibility that the Dick she has chosen to rebound with may actually not be "all that" even if he seems to be at the moment. When a man makes us feel beautiful and wanted, especially in the wake of another man's disinterest, we sometimes put on rose-colored glasses that later leave us wondering, "What the hell was I thinking?" Accept the fact that you probably weren't and be forgiving of yourself.

Breakups are hard, and there is no exact science to rebounding. So cut yourself some slack, collect and file the takeaways for future use, and celebrate the notion that you are now one step closer to finding the exact right Dick for you.

Remember, before you can kiss a Dick, you need to kiss a few frogs. That's just how the dating game works, unfortunately.

<u>Sex</u>
He came;
I cried;
He damn near died!

CHAPTER 13

DICK, JANE, AND THEIR MANY FRIENDS

I am not quite sure when exactly this whole "group dating" revolution actually took root, but it is a phenomenon that confounds me. I guess because I don't see the point in it.

Yes, I get the concept of getting together with a bunch of Janes, then meeting up with a bunch of Dicks to have a good time. That's a normal practice, especially among young adults. And certainly, Jane and Dick's spending one-on-one time together, otherwise known as a *date*, is also quite normal. What's odd to me, however, is how two very usual behaviors merged to become a style of dating that resembles more of a group chat than an actual date.

Adding to mine and many parents' bewilderment is that there seems to be no chronological cutoff for group dating. Men and women seem to be engaging in the practice all the way through their early 30s—

killing time while delaying marriage, I guess. Or might it be that group dating is actually hindering the marital objective? Because unless you plan on marrying everyone in the group, the opportunity to get to know one person for that very same intention is being severely limited by continuously group dating. Many Janes that I have spoken with say yes.

There is no doubt that the emergence of social media has propagated the group mentality. That said, there is a point when you need to check your friends at the door, cope with your social anxiety on your own the best that you can, and meet Dick all by your lonesome, and he needs to do the same. It is the only way you two are ever going to figure out if you should be carving your initials into the tree next to each other's or need to branch out further.

My advice would be to discontinue the practice of group dating by age twenty-five—no later. Beyond this point, the *maturity* and *respectability* of both Dick and Jane begin to be called into question. Additionally, Jane does need to keep in mind the very real limitations set forth by her biological clock if she wants to give birth someday.

Dating in group fashion won't help her here, whereas dating one Dick at a time, will. Better you set your life in motion and embrace your future rather than remain part of a group that keeps you clinging to the past and ten of your best buddies who are also stuck there. Life is much too valuable and fleeting for this.

CHAPTER 14

JANE'S FRIENDS ARE MAD

Good friends are a vital part of our lives and rare to find. We all know this. But sometimes they can be less than understanding when it comes to you dating a new Dick. They may seem to be on your side at first. Then, suddenly, play time is no longer the same and neither are *you* in their opinion. Dick becomes the enemy, and your friends become impediments to your happiness. Sound familiar?

The simple solution is merely to have patience with your friends while keeping Dick in first place in your life. True friends will come around, even if it means having a few uncomfortable but necessary conversations with them to ensure this. They need to be reminded that you do care but that Dick must take priority for the obvious reasons, none of which detract from how important they are or ever will be to you. If they still don't make the leap, place some distance between you and them and see what ultimately unfolds.

Even if Dick turns out to be a dud, knowing that you gave him and your dating life your all removes blame from anyone or anything else but the true culprit (whatever that may be). Your friends will eventually re-emerge, carrying with them supportive words and possibly a giggle, and, together, you will go on...until the next time, that is. It's a cycle—one that you will find yourself on the other side of, someday, when your friend meets her own monumental Dick.

What happens, however, if the Dick she finally settles upon is the very same one you, decidedly, left behind? Some Janes become crazed by the switch. Others could care less, their motto being, "Been there; done that."

In my opinion, the best way to resolve any potential issues arising between two Janes over one Dick is simply to communicate. As dating truly requires a certain amount of *responsibility* and *maturity*, so does resolving such matters. Being upfront will be easier on everyone, as will accepting and understanding your friend's current feelings and love interest. There's a great deal to being a good friend. "Selflessness" is necessity.

That said, try not to overreach when it comes to bypassing your gal pals for your Dick. If you are going to be spending a lot of time playing with him, you might just try including them in the fun every once in a while (outside of the bedroom, of course). Or plan an evening solely with them. We Janes need time with our friends, and any Dick worth his weight in salt will understand this, I assure you. Plus, the momentary distance between will make his heart grow fonder and yours too.

CHAPTER 15

JANE RIDES THE PONY

Most little girls want ponies, and so do most big girls—the more agreeable and steadfast, the better. That said, many girls don't want to share their ponies with any other Jane once they have them safely galloping about in one corral. And yet today, the idea of remaining fenced-in with a single Jane seems to leave many Dicks and their ponies cold, which certainly makes dating that much more difficult.

Let me be frank: If you are truly serious about dating with the intent of finding someone to love and possibly ride off into the sunset with, choosing a Dick who is ready to steer his pony towards your corral *only* is imperative. If you are not interested in this or believe that there is a better way than the advice I am giving you, ride the range as you please. Just make sure that everyone involved knows the score.

There are lots of women today who feel that sex is an equal-opportunity activity. They've redefined the sanctity of it as well as almost everything else about it. They've removed the limits and readdressed all of the rules, and for them, it has been freeing. But for many other Janes, it has not. In fact, it has bridled them to the point of their being called prudish and prevented them from finding men who portray any real desire to stick to one corral. The frustration these women are experiencing simply because they don't agree with the repackaging of sex is enormous, and so is the divide between these two groups. The only one who seems to be winning in this war is Dick, in my opinion, because he gets to have his oats and eat them too.

Now, I'm not here to judge either type of Jane... nor Dick for that matter. I do speak from experience, however, when I say that the personal value you place on sex directly correlates with the personal value a man places on you. This wisdom applies to dating as well as to larger commitments that may come down the line between the two of you.

So, although the old-time stigma associated with sleeping with as many Dicks as possible may have been curtailed or tossed over the fence completely by many of today's women, plenty of men still want to know that the woman they have decided to bring back to the homestead hasn't become a professional rodeo rider prior to their doing so.

Double standard? You betcha, but no less fair than the change in circumstances many Janes, who do not agree with current sexual trends, must cope with. I learned quite some time ago that as long as there are two people in any situation, both have a say in how things turn out. Dating and sex are no different, which is something to keep in mind on the larger scale and on the smaller. This includes while alone in the bedroom with Dick and, let's say, he surprises you by pulling out a whip.

Whether you say nay, bray, or urgently run away, being true to yourself needs to be your first priority. It will become his too if he really wants you, I promise. However, understand that certain sexual proclivities, such as whips, blinders, or even saddles, don't easily go away. If your Dick prefers this kind of romp and you don't, hightail it back to the range and find yourself another pony. You will both ultimately be much happier, and don't let the words "I love you" change your mind. It's sheer *horseshit* when it arrives at the end of a branding.

Personally, I still don't understand what the point is in rushing to have sex when dating. This isn't to say that I don't understand a woman's natural sexual urges. The fact that I have five kids and am not Mormon speaks for itself. However, so does a woman's ability to be discriminating as well as respectful of her body and self-worth.

When a woman is able to hold back from having sex too early when dating a man, she forces him to make a decision to either stick around and get to know her or not. If Dick truly likes her, he will stay put and wait until she finally agrees to have sex with him. If he does not, he will find another Jane. The decision to have or not to have sex incorporates a ready-made insurance policy for Jane.

Why give that up just because you can't or don't want to lasso your own sex drive? I've known many women who found themselves lying face-down in the mud because they thought the ride of their lives would end up in "happily ever after" only to learn otherwise. They ended up feeling terrible about themselves and disgusted by their Dicks.

Now approaching their late 20s and early 30s and no closer to marriage than on the day they first began to date, these Janes regret boarding the Pony Express years earlier. Today, given the choice again, they would have taken the slow route to the stables instead of the one that led them to where they currently find themselves—out to pasture.

CHAPTER 16

JANE LIKES TWO PONIES

I think it is perfectly acceptable for a woman to date two men at the same time, provided she has the ability to juggle Dicks ably and that both men clearly understand that they are not alone. The competition will definitely bring out the best in them and certainly lend itself to figuring out which Dick is more suited to Jane more quickly.

I do not, however, recommend riding either pony while continuing to date both Dicks in tandem. Neither will appreciate it, and there is no benefit to turning your dating life into a hoedown fraught with confusion and, probably, rumor.

I will be the first to admit that it is fun to date, especially at the beginning, when the world feels like your oyster and there is a never-ending flow of available men to choose from. But once you start moving up in years, the quality and number of great guys who are also single takes a downward turn, leaving many Janes disenchanted with the entire process.

This is the reason why, as you date, it is important to remember why you are doing so. If you are merely marking time, then mark away with those Dicks who feel the same. But if you are dating with the goal of marriage in mind, then date with a conscience, because the last thing you want to do is to have a ton of fun today, then wake up in the future wishing you had been more serious about the entire endeavor. You don't want to look back and say, "Boy, what an idiot I was to let that Dick get away." Living in regret is no fun for anyone, so better you keep your eye on the ball as you discern which Dick is the right one for you.

Most women find that when they do spend some time alternating between Dicks, realizing which among them is the winner becomes acutely clear almost immediately. If it does not, Jane may be experiencing some sort of internal struggle that is keeping her from reconfiguring the dynamic. Or, she may not have found her match in either of them and needs to seek out a better-suited Dick, one who embodies pieces of both to create the perfect whole.

If this is the case, continuing to date for the sake of becoming more attuned to what kind of Dick you are looking for while enjoying the excitement of being out and about town is exactly what you should be doing. For others who are tired of the search, taking breaks from dating now and again can be therapeutic and a necessary part of reigniting your desire to find someone.

I know of many Janes who spend their evenings perusing dating websites in order to dip their toes back in the proverbial dating pool without becoming fully immersed. So worn out are they by the dating scene that they just can't bring themselves to jump back in again. Eventually, however, they see a handsome face that coerces them to reopen the door...and then they see another. Before long, they find themselves dining at the same restaurant twice in one week, waiting to see if the same waiter they had yesterday will reveal their dirty little secret. Dating websites are hotbeds for dating overload. They are also respectable ways for busy men and women to meet and date.

Ultimately, demonstrating good character is the key to dating responsibly and effectively, no matter how many Dicks escort you to your favorite watering hole or stare down the waiter who seems to understand you without even so much as a whisper.

CHAPTER 17
DICK READS BOOKS, NOT MINDS

"**H**ow could he have not known this?" It is a familiar question all women find themselves asking when dating men whom they have confused with telepaths. Somehow we get the insane notion stuck in our heads that along with all the perks of dating us, men acquire the supernatural ability to read our minds as well.

I'm not quite sure how we make that connection, but we do. Then, suddenly, we find out otherwise, transforming our level ground into shaky territory and our near-perfect dating life into something that resembles reality and requires effort. Oh no!

Men will be the first to admit that they don't read minds. In fact, if ever you queried every man on the planet as to whether he **could** or **couldn't** read minds, every one of them would shout "couldn't" followed by the statement "I'm sorry," because that is what they have become accustomed to saying at the hands of our own misconception. I feel for them, and I really believe we Janes can do better to eliminate the issues caused by expecting men to mind-read when they can't.

This means that if he suggests taking you to a movie, the main actor of which you hate, tell him and work together on an alternate plan. He will appreciate it. You will appreciate it. And the evening won't be bogged down by suppositions that could have been avoided had you truly given him a fair shot at being "super" natural.

There is no correlation between being right for each other and being able to read each other's minds. Yes, as couples evolve, they get better at recognizing cues and understanding their partner's likes and dislikes, wants and needs. But that's not you yet. Your partner can't possibly know what would be required to even get close to reading your mind in all of three months of dating you, so don't expect it of him.

Expecting his best and giving him the chance to please you as your dating life evolves are all that you can ask of him and give him at this stage of the game. You will undoubtedly trip him up and sabotage your mutual happiness if you go for more. *Overasking* on your part will most definitely result in *underachieving* on his.

As two people who are in this dating relationship together, it is important for you both to give each other, and the time you choose to spend together, a fair shake. To do this, you need to drop all notions that Dick can read your mind so that you can allow the very plausible possibility of his learning to read (and keep) your heart.

CHAPTER 18

JANE EXAMINES HERSELF

Over the course of the initial three months of dating, it is important for Jane to check in with herself periodically to discern whether or not she is happy with her particular Dick, including what attracted her to him in the first place. Doing this will help her understand herself better as well as figure out what she wants from this dating relationship going forward.

Undoubtedly, chemistry will occupy a portion of her answer, but what that word actually means can be tricky. I know that the chemistry that prompted me to date the man I eventually married was very different from the chemistry that compelled me to date the rock star years later, following my husband's death. I wanted two different things from these men, and had both arrived at other times in my life, I might not have been attracted to either.

Suffice it to say, there is more to chemistry than just an internal push towards one Dick over another. It is ultimately composed of a mixture of several elements, making it a very fickle master. This is the reason that *checking in* with yourself on occasion is so beneficial. It will help to validate first impressions, review expectations, and determine where you are currently sitting on the happiness scale.

For instance, if all you had planned upon when meeting your Dick was to "slum it" for a few weeks, but now you feel as if he is falling in love with you, you need to look at this and take the space required to decide how you want to proceed. Alternately, if you were bowled over by your Dick from the start and began seeing butterflies and rainbows early on in your dating life together, you need to get a handle on this too.

It is important to stay in tune with how you're feeling, where you are going, and how he fits in, especially the more you learn about each other. There is so much you two need to be in sync with to successfully consider moving to the next stage of dating. Chemistry won't sustain a relationship for very long. Like a match, it can light the fire, but it will burn out quickly if other, less romantic, elements are not in place, including agreeable personalities, shared goals, and the ability to meld lives without killing each other in the process.

There is no doubt that opposites may experience explosive chemistry together initially, but most, when involved in committed relationships, will part ways eventually, leaving them to wonder what they ever saw in each other. Chemistry might have entranced them, but it could not keep them together, which brings up another aspect of the little devil.

Chemistry can become a harmful trap, chaining many a Jane to a Dick she does not deserve. Yet somehow she just can't break free. I've seen this type of behavior, the consequences of which span everything from an aching heart to an ailing backside. And although I understand how powerful chemistry can be, I also believe that women are very special beings who have the capacity to overcome just about anything put before them. Blame it on chemistry? I think not.

As chemistry can be confusing, blinding, and even troublesome at times, it can also be thrilling and enormously beneficial to the evolution of your dating life as well as yourself. For some Janes, the right chemistry will awaken them to aspects of themselves they never knew existed. It will expand their worlds and make them feel more alive, happy, and inspired than ever before. Life will seem almost perfect, except for the occasional passing doubt that this bliss—and for that matter, Dick—is just too good to be true.

The practice of *checking in* with yourself every now and again will help to keep such absurdities at bay while preventing you from losing your grip on reality altogether. We all know what it feels like to be mesmerized by a magnificent Dick. It can take a bit of doing to come back to one's senses. "Better you stay put for a while once you do" is what I say, at least until you find your head again in light of the magnetic nature of Dick's.

Money

He paid;
I laid;
We stayed.

I paid;
He laid;
We dead!

CHAPTER 19

DICK NEEDS A MAKEOVER

I'm not quite sure why certain women feel the need to alter men from the guys they present themselves to be in the onset of dating. At what point did these Janes conclude that the individuals who obviously caught their attention in the first place needed to be remade? I personally would feel offended. How would Jane like it if Dick told her that she was unacceptable in current form? She wouldn't take it too well, I imagine.

No one likes to be told that they are subpar. Superheroes may seem bulletproof, but even they view this type of criticism as harsh and unjust. Men are not women and never will be. We need to stop criticizing them for their masculine ways.

If you are choosing a man, I recommend you relish him for all of the individual and gender differences as well as exceptional qualities he brings to the dating relationship. In embracing what makes your Dick unique (and both of you *unique* together), you ultimately create a better whole and a ton of possibilities for fun and future.

I loved knowing that my late husband had strengths that I did not. I adored our many differences, as they helped to broaden my world. Plus, I appreciated the comfort of knowing that if the roof caved in, he could fix it. Change him? What an absurd thought that would have never occurred to me. I can, however, understand how it does to many women, those who have yet to age into such experience and wisdom. When a Jane is too young to know which battles to fight and which to accept for the good of the whole, one mistake on the part of her Dick can lead her to weigh the need for an entire overhaul of him.

Men are designed not to be like us because they were given very different jobs to do. And regardless of today's constant screaming and aggressive reinterpretation of what men "should" be, most are doing exceptionally well at fulfilling the roles they were meant to play and more.

Instead of harping on them for not being women, we Janes really need to be grateful that they are their own unique selves. Frankly, I don't want to sleep with a duplicate of me, no matter how entertaining I am during the day. Nor do I believe that women have the right to project imperfections onto men that don't exist just because they are different from us. It's a bit self-righteous, if you ask me, and not at all fair. Nor is it consistent with the current mindset that everyone has the right to be who they are. What makes this different?

Take my advice: If you give your Dick the space to be himself during the first three months of dating and every new month thereafter, you won't regret it. You may not always understand him, but so what? That would happen anyway, merely because we are not just different genders but because we are individuals too. Plus, a little mystery adds to the excitement and romance of dating, whereas picking on him doesn't.

If after a few dates, you decide that your Dick is just not for you because he wears his differences poorly or your personalities just don't match up, you can always resume the search for another Dick more your speed and revel in the knowledge that you gave this one a good try. Dating is an exercise of trial and error. So appreciate the lesson learned and move on.

CHAPTER 20

DICK LOSES HIS BALLS

It befuddles me how readily *gentlemanly* behavior gets misinterpreted by so many young women today. Instead of viewing these respect-filled gestures in the true manner in which they are being offered, Janes are seeing these acts as denigrating and meeting them with unbridled hostility, which stumps me yet again. Whoever said that one bad turn deserves another, given that this is how these actions are being viewed?

It seems to me that the real assault, in these cases, is upon the thoughtful guy going out of his way to be considerate to the Jane who is hitting him over the head for it. With everything today up for public scrutiny, men are under fire for displaying the very same manners that they would have been shot for not displaying a few short years ago. Pretty damn frustrating for them, if you ask me, as well as for the responsible parents who spent time reinforcing this behavior in their sons.

As there is the propensity to twist just about everything uttered today into a pretzel for all kinds of reasons, many of which blow my mind, the admirable act of 'a man opening a door for a woman' seems to have become some sort of battle cry for certain Janes concerned with turning the clock backward on equality—as if uttering a proper "thank you" would strip us of the rights bequeathed to us under the 19th Amendment or something. I assure you, it won't. Although screaming at a guy who considerately pulls out your chair may make some question if you personally have regressed to an earlier time.

Modern men are not idiots. Most are extremely aware of how strong, intelligent, and capable women are—especially those who behave as *gentlemen* around them. Their show of manners should not be designated as a sign of deprecation but of reverence for every Jane in the room. Taking it any other way is an insult to the intelligence of these men and a real affront to our gender as a whole.

In other words, stop yelling at men who are displaying good character and show some of your own by handling these situations in ways that truly support what you preach. Nobody is going to accuse you of being weak if you allow Dick to carry your groceries up the stairs. In fact, most will admire you for the powerful impression you've left on him, the one that instigated such attentive behavior.

It is not easy being a man in this world today. Caught up in our own concerns, we Janes have the propensity to overlook this. There is a great deal of mixed messaging going on, forcing men to "man up" in ways they have never had to before. We are pantsing them at every turn, forcing them to assimilate, and leaving no real bastion for them to run to, just because we don't want to be viewed as the weaker sex. Doesn't sound particularly fair, and it's certainly not in our best interest, unless, of course, we are all willing to go around carrying our own groceries for the rest of our lives. It's something to think about the next time you reach for the car door handle prior to exiting his Honda. In other words, let him open it.

All in all, whether you are seeking a gentleman in your life or not, there are better ways to communicate than through aggression. Cutting Dick's balls off won't positively impact the way society views and treats women. Nor will it inspire him to continue to date you.

Piss him off and make him rue the day he ever laid eyes on you? That's probably more like what you can expect...and deserve.

CHAPTER 21

DICK OPENS HIS PIGGY BANK

OK, so riddle me this. How does paying for your own meal while out on a date represent progress for anyone but possibly the smart bastard who coaxed you into such a ridiculous arrangement? I really want to know, because the answer escapes me.

For years, men have been finding the resources to take women out, be it to dinner, the movies, concerts, sporting events, etc. But today, for some reason, women feel the need to worry about whether or not the check will be split at the end of an evening, which compels me to ask the question, "Do you think supermodels ever entertain such a worry?" I think not, and neither should you. Your life is just as valuable and meaningful as theirs, Jane. They just believe it, and men pay for the company, the beauty, and the opportunity to sit next to that confidence.

Frankly, a man who takes you to dinner already assumes you are a woman worthy of spending a few bucks on, otherwise he would not break open his wallet, I assure you. Offering to pay for your own fish kabob does nothing but save him a few dollars and make him question his choice in catches. He doesn't go into the evening thinking you can't pay for yourself. He goes into the evening thinking how he is going to prove to you that you should get to know him so that he can eventually sleep with you. That's reality, ladies. The only statement you are making by offering to go halfsies is that you might not actually be "all that."

So let me just say it plainly. Stop offering to pay for your own dinner when a man takes *you* out. The minute you open your wallet will be the first of many times you will do so, I assure you, whether when dating or over the course of a lifetime, if things get that far. The minimum a man should do is be able to pay for your meal. If he can't, I'm not quite sure why he would be attractive to you, because you can't tell me that he makes you feel special. And you can't tell me that he's building confidence in you for the long haul, given he can't even fund a dinner between the two of you today.

Dating is not a Dutch activity unless you both live in the Netherlands. Thus, you should cement the thought into your head, before you even respond to an invitation, that you are not the one in the equation who is going to pay, Jane. If you feel it is a concern in the onset, either don't dine with him or make your intentions known before you leave your abode so that he can be clear on your expectations. Behave as a grown-up, I say, just as you want him to do. Grown men front the bill, and grown women accept what these men can give and then thank them for it. If you are unhappy with what a particular Dick has to offer, refuse his invitation and choose another Dick to spend the evening with.

There are plenty of women in this world who are happy with this exchange. None of them, however, would even crack a smile at the possibility of having to open their purses when out with a man. And no, this does not make them whores, paid escorts or anything similarly vulgar in nature. It makes them smart, because they know that there is security in their being able to rely on Dick to bring home the bacon on the off chance that they don't want to, can't or prefer not to "do it all" while raising a family. Women are practical that way, throughout most of the world, that is. They hope for the best and plan for the worst.

As far as you're concerned, when Dick comes a-callin' he should envision you as dirt poor, then ask himself the question, "Do I want this woman anyway?" His answer will reveal a lot about him, you, and the couple you will be together. If you discover that you both had the best time of your lives sharing a hero sandwich and watching the moon from a park bench somewhere, that says an awful lot. Alternately, if you felt cheated because he took you out for a fancy meal and then forgot to order up ice cream at the end...well, that says something completely different and nothing good.

Money is not the great equalizer between men and women who are dating. I once had a man plan an entire vacation around the fact that he thought, by his asking me to go with him, that I would kick in some cash. His plans were magnificent, until he learned that I had no intention of paying for my side of the bed. He abruptly cancelled everything, then endeavored to make me feel guilty for not stepping up to the plate. And so I agreed, but not in the way that he expected. I line-drived him out of my life and shut down the long term relationship possibility altogether. I later met another gentleman who would come to refer to me as "the most inexpensive date he ever met." He never asked for a dime, and I never asked him for more than he could give. A simple coffee was just as much fun with him as a night out on the town. I was content with both because I was content with him.

This isn't to say, Jane, that if you invite a man out to dinner or an event, once you are dating for a while, that you don't pay for him. If you are doing the inviting, you should also do the paying, just as he should balk at allowing you to carry through on your offer or should reject it entirely...which only means that you insist until one of you wins the debate. I'm not implying that you have no financial responsibility when dating Dick. Buying him thoughtful presents beyond just his birthday or holiday gifts, using your resources to make him knick-knacks or treats he loves, and cooking him dinner (if that is something you know he likes) should all be part of your regular contribution to your dating life, as should occasionally arranging for an unexpected, somewhat costly outing. But the *big money* expenditures should be saved for when you are committed to a full-fledged relationship with future plans on the horizon. You will kick yourself if you do it any other way.

Now, mind you, once you have established that your piggy bank is off-limits, if your Dick is not Mr. Moneybags, you will probably be subject to a ton of creative dating ideas, which can be a great deal of fun and a good indication of what your future might look like if you happen to marry this Dick and have kids together. Chances are, when the "bundles of joy" come, the cash leaves. Enjoying simple, inexpensive evenings together is a must, whether out or in.

My late husband used to arrange "adventures" for us before we had our four children and also thereafter. They spanned everything from picnicking on the cliffs of the Hudson River to perusing a very eclectic, messy, and charming bookstore we grew to adore in Nyack, New York, then chowing down on cookies and cappuccino at the local bakery to sustain us. Both were romantic and both were memorable. Never once did he ask me to chip in, and this consideration and respect went a long way with me. Knowing that he would do anything to take care of me made me feel the same towards him...and I did till the day that he died and well beyond through the care I put into fostering his legacy.

You see, if you don't get it already, the most important part of Dick's paying for your dinner is the sacrifice he is making in doing so. We all realize that money does not come easily...to anyone. So if he is spending his on you, he is stating something pretty significant through his sacrifice. If he is not, he's stating something completely different but equally as strong. Don't you think it is smarter to know what he's actually stating before you go ahead and break open your own piggy bank?

Hold on to your quarters until he makes his intentions known and you agree with them. I promise you, he would do the same if he had that option, Jane. He already has, to the chagrin of one too many foreboding women and their empty pocketbooks. Losing an emotional investment is tough enough without compounding it financially too.

That's savvy investment speak for, "Don't get caught with your own pants down, unless he is willing to pay for them!"

CHAPTER 22
JANE HAS A SECRET

There is a phrase that I used in the previous chapter that might just set off a plethora of alarms. I anticipate so, actually. The phrase is "take care of me." I doubt I really need to explain why, as we Janes are all familiar with the ridicule that goes along with wanting to be "taken care of" by our Dicks. And yet, the truth is, most of us do.

My personal belief is that we are programmed to want this because, years ago, when it took all we had to merely survive, having Dick take care of Jane allowed Jane to take care of the cubs (so to speak) and that dynamic proved rather foolproof, which is why it still lives in us today. Whether or not times have changed has no bearing on the conversation going on within our heads that we have no say over. The fact is, our conscious mind is not always in control. Sometimes we need to redirect it to adapt to present-day standards.

There is no doubt that women are certainly capable of taking care of themselves, and that we are getting better at doing so daily. This truth, however, does not mean that our desire to want a man to be able to or actually embrace 'taking care of us' is invalid or extinct. It means that it still exists for many of us but that we've learned to adapt to current societal norms; each adaptation falling somewhere between staying home full-time and running a multimillion-dollar corporation—whatever floats your boat and makes your life work, is what I say. Neither is wrong.

"Wrong" happens when a woman is denounced for her personal choices or her honesty in admitting that she wants a man to take care of her. No one has the right to pass such harsh judgment, especially if you do not walk in this Jane's Mary Janes. I believe that our gender is strong enough to embrace all options without killing each other in the process, although there are moments when I find myself disheartened by the unnecessary bickering over the matter between some Janes. We live in a great big world, folks—there is space enough for everyone, including the men who purposely seek out women to date who will allow them the privilege of caring for them financially. And they are out there, just as their counterparts are as well.

Regardless of your personal preferences here, when dating, you need to realize the profound obligation of caring for another human being that you are inviting into your life. Unless you are dating just for fun—shunning any strings that might come down the line—dating means that you are now inviting the responsibility of caring for another into your life. Essential to this is caring for that person in the way you would like to be cared for as well. Even limiting the financial contribution made initially, as per my prior recommendation, you need to make yourself available to your date emotionally, intellectually, and physically, otherwise there is nothing to be gained from the experience and no future ahead if that is what the two of you want. He must also do the same for you.

What I am getting at is that the negative connotation that has been tacked onto the phrase "I want to be taken care of," as desired by many women, is misguided because it undermines the intimacy, beauty, and reality of the union between Dick and Jane at every stage. If you are set on dating, you will be taking care of Dick's needs as much as he will be taking care of yours. If one of those needs for some Janes includes financial security, don't shame them for it. Admire them for knowing what they want and allow them to do the same for you.

As there is a cover for every pot, Jane, there is no need for us pots to call any kettles black. It's just bad character and does not bode well for our gender overall, I'm afraid. Makes us look like foolish little girls.

CHAPTER 23

DICK AND JANE CONNECT

The biggest compliment a man can offer a woman is to say, "You get me." Why? Because that type of connection is extremely rare, especially given the impenetrable wall of masculinity most men keep up.

Dick or Jane, we need to feel understood to substantiate why the hell we are on this planet to begin with, otherwise we are destined to feel lost and alone. The elusive and precious "human connection" is more than a *male-female* thing; if two people find it, they usually guard it with their lives. We know when something is special and not to be squandered. Well, most of us do, anyway. There are those few cases made up of men and women who piss all over a flower garden only to wonder why the tulips died. Hopefully, that is not you.

In any event, one of the blissful realities of truly connecting with your Dick is how natural the flow is between the two of you, which includes conversation, scheduling time together, and basically everything else that comes down the line, minus a few hiccups. Your sync just can't be beat, and the joy that comes from this, including between the sheets when that moment arrives, is self-generating. Dick and Jane may not be the same, but when they have exceptional flow, it delivers them to the closest realm they are ever going to get to being so. They may even actually feel as if they *do* share one brain at times.

When your connection with Dick occurs freely and easily, all of the attributes that make for a strong and supportive bond between you two come together. You want to be kind; you want to be thoughtful; you want to rearrange your schedule so that you can spend an additional hour in each other's company. You want to buy him tokens of affection, because the idea of not... that becomes foreign to you rather quickly.

Dick and the dating relationship begin to take first place in your mind (and heart...let's be honest). Then, before you know it, you become each other's reason for being and your dating relationship moves to a deeper level, and now, most definitely, into the bedroom, where you probably experience the most mind-blowing sex of your life. You know what they say, "If it is good outside the bedroom; it will be good inside it too," especially under the circumstances of which I speak.

Feeling connected to someone is the best feeling in the world and should never be taken for granted, even during times of trouble. It can carry you through a lot together and lay the groundwork for an amazing future between you. The downside is that it can also wound you in ways that some Dicks and Janes never recover from, if in fact the relationship fractures or you split up totally.

Unfortunately (and fortunately), once you are involved in this kind of connection, you can't help but become swept up in it, so be cognizant of this prior to agreeing to dip your toe in the water. It is not for the faint of heart, but it will require you to give your entire heart over if you discover that you are one of the lucky few. Be prepared, Jane, because the time to back out ain't after the first date. It's before. No life preserver is going to save you after that.

Choose wisely when you have the chance and expect the plunge to be monumental, wherever it leads. Great flow is, in itself, its own best teacher...and the least forgiving.

CHAPTER 24

JANE SITS ON A PEDESTAL

They say that every Jane should date the Dick who feels like he is dating "up." The reason is that he will always treat her like gold for fear of losing her otherwise. I believe this to be true, as I have experienced it in my own life as well. If a man thinks he's won a prize in your agreeing to go out with him, he won't disappoint, I assure you. The notion that he will never find another girl better than you is enough to keep him on his toes throughout all of dating and, for some men, forever. His dating up, however, does not imply that you are dating "down." It just means that he's placed you on a pedestal, even though you may be equally wowed by him.

When it comes to the man Jane should choose, however, I would recommend she find the man that she "can't live without" rather than the one she can easily live *with*. It's even better if that Dick is one and the same.

I am a big believer in practicality, folks, and I don't think there is anything practical about dating a guy who doesn't tickle your fancy to the point of insanity. Life is too short to settle for anything less. Unfortunately, too many women learn this lesson the hard way. They date, then marry, the practical guy, whom they share a decent love with but no real passion for. Twenty years later, they hit the wall, unable to suffer his touch another day or endure feeling unfulfilled and alone any longer. They want out and thus, divorce proceedings begin.

There is no doubt that society influences women to look for certain characteristics in a partner—good looks, money, a likeable demeanor, athletically inclined, an impressive education, and a stellar résumé. Not one of these things, however, has anything to do with finding and falling in deep and profound love—the type of love that makes no sense at all and drives you to do crazy things that surprise even you (like drawing the doodle of you and him standing on the top of a wedding cake...you know, that one)!

There is a big difference between dating a guy because he looks good on paper and dating a guy because he looks good to you for an inexplicable reason that you can neither express nor get around. The guy I am describing is the one who keeps you up at night. He's the Dick, Jane, whom you should date, because he's the one who will truly change your life.

Now, I say this maintaining the assumption that he is a relatively normal guy who doesn't harbor any truly destructive habits or behaviors and has his shit together for the most part. Given all this is true, jump on the back of his two-wheeler and pedal forward, because this is the type of coupling romance novels are made of. I speak from experience, and I wouldn't have traded that experience for the world. It still lives in me today.

You never forget a love like that or the many dates that led up to it. They become irreplaceable memories that shape your very existence. And even if the dating comes to an end (for whatever reason), you'll know in your heart that this single person gave you an irreplaceable gift and for that, you will be eternally grateful.

For some older people, this type of loss will trigger a depth of grief that they just can't bounce back from. We all know the wife who dies days after her husband passes away or vice versa. **Death by a broken heart** is what they call it. No one wants to die, but since we all have to, is there any better way to go? I think not.

Does this mean that, by choosing this Dick, you can expect a perfect human being, that he will never disappoint you and you will never have a fight? Absolutely not. But the same could be true given you choose a practical Dick instead. What you get with this Dick is the glue that drives you to forgive him even when you want to kill him (metaphorically, of course); he's the one who won't allow you to give up on him so easily or at all. He becomes your reason for being and you, his.

To shortchange yourself of this by choosing the safer Dick might result in a few more pennies in your piggy bank but potentially could bankrupt you inside. You can always make money, I say. Encounter and date the Dick who forces you to rethink everything you ever thought about life and love? Much more difficult. Don't let the possibilities pass you by, Jane. Heed my words to avoid living a life of regret.

<u>Procreation</u>

My mom said, "Go";
My dad said no;
And now I'm tyin' a baby bow.

CHAPTER 25

JANE PATS THE BALL

Of course, you know when you meet the Dick whom you can't live without, sex may take on a whole new meaning for you. You probably will be surprised at the intense focus you will have on bedroom opportunities and activities and may even discover a whole new side of you made up of cravings and requests that have never accompanied you between the sheets before. My advice is to 'go with it' and prepare for a ton of self-discovery and fun. Remember, the enormous pleasure sex brings isn't only for him. It is just as important for you, and you should both see it this way. For women who are still virgins, this is the type of situation that will most likely change that status. Applaud your fortitude for remaining true to your moral code but understand that some things, you just can't fight.

That said, if you do decide to refrain from having sex with Dick and can manage that magnitude of restraint, make sure that you make your decision completely clear to him, especially since his desire to play ball with you might feel uncontrollable at times. Any mixed messaging may cause a great thing to go unexpectedly and tragically awry.

As one in five women is raped during her lifetime, according to the Centers for Disease Control and Prevention, you need to be conscious of this when dating, especially when you are young and fairly new at it. Although rape definitely does not discriminate according to age, young women tend to lack the communication skills and confidence that mature women have developed. This puts them at a disadvantage when communicating their intentions about sex with a date, especially one jacked-up already or intent on his own agenda. Even the nice Dick has a tough time restraining himself when he likes a woman, but he does restrain himself, because he respects her will and doesn't want to wear an orange jumpsuit for the next 20 years of his life.

As we are living in extremely frustrating and violent times underscored by more freedom than ever before, men and women are facing and feeling the impact of this, and the results can be very scary for single women out on dates or involved in dating relationships. They have to be more guarded and be more aware than ever before while establishing guidelines for themselves and absolute clarity with Dick. In other words, women who date today need to err on the side of caution, always!

Recently, one of my daughters shared a story about a friend who placed herself in a dangerous situation with a date that led the girl to be raped after consuming a combination of Red Bull and rum. Her heart pounding intensely from the physical effects of such a concoction, coupled with the panic, fear, and shock of enduring such a violent act, the girl believed she would surely die. She didn't, but a piece of her did that day, and it will be a hard-won fight for her to ever return to any type of normalcy with regards to sex and intimacy again.

Did this girl place herself in the position where she made the initial mistake that opened herself up to being raped? The answer is yes. But mistakes and misjudgements happen, especially when dating. We are only human, and reality speaks that a woman's lapse in judgement should in no way be perceived as an invitation to be abused or violently attacked, whether sex is involved or not.

We don't live in a safe world. So if you are going to date, be prepared to defend yourself in case it is ever required. Take the self-defense courses available today. Keep aware of trends that are occurring within the dating culture. Listen to the news so that you know what the heck is going on in your neck of the woods and overall. And take some time to visualize what you would do and the lengths you would be willing to go to defend yourself if indeed you experience date rape. Doing all of these things will help you prevent or handle such an encounter more ably than if you don't. And, please, if you are raped or sustain a violent act of any kind, report it! You do no one a favor by keeping silent.

I have to say, I am floored by how many women today don't understand what constitutes a violent act in dating or overall. Allow me to define it with the World Health Organization's help: Violence is "the intentional use of physical force or power, threatened or actual, against oneself, another person, or against a group or community, which either results in or has a high likelihood of resulting in injury, death, psychological harm, maldevelopment, or deprivation." In other words, if it doesn't feel right, it's wrong, especially if it makes you feel uncomfortable or sends you into a state of fear or panic, which in turn compels you to think, motion or voice the word "no." I say this, however, assuming that you will apply common sense to these situations as well.

For instance, if you happen to be frightened of puppies and your date arrives to your door with his because he proudly wants to show you the adorable critter, your hysterical response combined with his lack of agreement to take the dog back home just yet doesn't constitute a violent act against you. It simply means that he loves his puppy and is hoping that, with a little gentle encouragement and time, your irrational fear will dissipate and you will come to appreciate the little fella too. I realize this example may be stretching it a bit, but you get my drift.

Without delving too much deeper into this topic, as dating Dick can result in a lot of things, your time with him should never result in your feeling violated, angry or hurt, physically or otherwise. If it does, you have the right to protect yourself and every other woman that may come after you in his life. In fact, consider it your responsibility and act accordingly.

CHAPTER 26

JANE ASKS SALLY WHAT TO DO

As dating is an activity driven more by emotion than intellect, it can be tough sometimes to make good decisions while doing it. We all know the girl who continuously chooses the bad boy, then wonders why her dating life feels more like a roller coaster than a merry-go-round. She ignores the advice from all of her friends, her family, and even Sally (the most reliable gal pal she has) only to experience the disappointment of all of them being right and her being both wrong and alone...again!

It's a painful cycle to watch or, worse yet, be at the center of, which is the reason it is vitally important that you do listen to and heed the advice of those who care about you when dating, especially your own personal Sally. No, I am not talking about the one girlfriend in your life who you are 'tied to the hip' to, as irreplaceable as she may be. I'm talking about the voice inside you who's been earnestly watching over you and guiding you since the moment you took your first breath. This little lady is Sally and she's been occupying a space inside all of us Janes since we began skipping across the planet.

Sally is amazing, as the speed and accuracy she has in producing the right answer for women to rely on cannot be beat. She's infallible as well as all-natural, unlike her copycat sisters Siri and Cortana, and you don't have to worry about misplacing her, as she remains permanently affixed where she began—and is devoted to you beyond belief.

Sally is indispensable to our dating lives because she always knows the right way to go. The more that we listen to her, the better we become at dating and not screwing up a good thing when it smacks us in the face and invites us to dinner.

She's the only part of us that can't break under any type of strain; in fact, she just becomes stronger and louder when things aren't right and you refuse to listen. The biggest impediment she faces in ensuring that we Janes all find our individual 'happily ever afters' is *us*.

When a woman refuses to listen to her Sally because what she's shouting from the rooftop does not jibe with the storyline that is playing out in her head about a particular Dick, you can bet your booty that the story will end more in horror than in love. This is the reason it is critical to listen to Sally even when she isn't saying what you want to hear. Her interest is in protecting you...your own personal bodyguard whom you really do need to respect when dating.

She's not there to throw stumbling blocks in your way but to remove them so that you will ultimately find the perfect Dick who will carry you off into the sunset without burning you along the way. Don't cast her aside, ever, as she will be the one you thank when you finally do meet that Dick whom you might just have looked past had she not shaken you back to your senses when he made that out-of-the-blue phone call telling you how amazing you are.

Be grateful for her. Give her words enormous deference. And remember that she only wants the best for you while you are also trying to find it for yourself. She can see beyond you and will tell you everything you need to know if you choose to listen.

CHAPTER 27

DICK AND JANE MEET THE PARENTS

We all go through a phase when we believe our parents are stupid. It is part of the growing-up process and usually strikes the hardest just around the time that we begin dating. Unfortunate but true, as their wisdom could cut down on a tremendous amount of turmoil, mistakes, and regret that occur at the hands of our own naiveté. Oh well. We do grow out of it eventually and realize that the only stupid person in the room at the time was us.

Parents can offer enormous insight into dating as well as your choice in Dicks. The fact is, although dating practices may have changed a bit and Dicks may have evolved too, the basic makeup of Dick has not, so helping to understand him is something your parents can easily do. They've been around for a long time. They've seen it all, and you? Not even close. You could use the help even if you swear you are just that much more savvy than they are, which does not mean that anyone thinks you are unintelligent. It just means that nothing can trump experience, and you don't have it!

With that said, allow me to suggest that if you are given the opportunity to bring your new Dick home to meet your parents before investing too much time in him, do so. Conversely, if he has the mind to invite you home sooner rather than later as well, accept his invitation and go. It's a great way to find out rather quickly if this Dick passes muster with two of the most important people in your life who have no other interest but your happiness. If he has some significant flaws that you are overlooking or behaves like a fish out of water when meeting them (outside of the normal nervousness), they will help you to see this so that you can then continue forward in a more informed state. Or they may absolutely love him, which could make you love him even more, something that would benefit the relationship entirely. Additionally, your Dick will be given ample opportunity to learn who they are and whether or not their relationship together, the one they have with you, and the life you grew up in delight him or detract from his attraction to you. Same goes for you when you meet his parents.

As family is an important part of most people's lives, gelling with each other's is a must. Frankly, they ain't goin' anywhere (with few exceptions), so it is better to share that part of your life on the early side rather than cement your relationship with the man of your dreams and then introduce him to the folks, as you could be preventing a nightmare from occurring.

Doing this will also allow you to see how your man's father treats his wife as well as how your Dick treats his mother. The rule of thumb is that if Dad and son treat Mom like gold, expect to be treated the same. The opposite is true as well, by the way. We learn from our parents, and this is one lesson you want to make sure he has right before he locks you into anything more serious. It makes all the difference, believe me. *Respect* and *caring* won't magically appear in your relationship or stick around if he has not seen it demonstrated between his parents. So don't fool yourself into thinking otherwise.

In being proactive in your introductions, I am in no way suggesting that your parents know everything that you need. Plenty of children choose partners who were pooh-poohed by their parents initially, only to prove their parents wrong. Our individual needs and preferences do count for something. Still, there are many others who find out they should have listened.

What I am saying is that it can't hurt to get an experienced and qualified second opinion from those who love you before you and Dick become inseparable. And imagine the brownie points each of you will win with *the* parents if you show such stellar judgment by inviting their opinions so early on in the game. Not only will they welcome the opportunity, but they will recognize your newfound level of maturity. Whether or not your parents fall in love with Dick, they will certainly pat themselves and you on the back for such solid thinking, fostering more faith in your decision-making ability in the future. It's a win-win for you either way.

One final thought, for all of you who hold no respect for your parents' opinions on dating, relationships or love interests in general because, in your eyes, they've screwed up their own lives with regards, I urge you to reconsider. Sometimes you can learn the most from the wisdom found in other's mistakes. Consider this before you write your parents' thoughts and insights off completely, especially as most parents only want the best for their kids.

CHAPTER 28

JANE'S FRIENDS LIKE DICK

Beyond being vetted by your parents, it is vitally important that the rest of your family and friends feel comfortable around your Dick too. It seems like it is asking a lot, and certainly, there are always one or two individuals in your life who will probably not agree with your decision for whatever reason. Being able to please everyone is a fallacy but wanting to receive a giant thumbs-up from most of the people you call "home" is understandable because it is vital that your Dick fits into your social circle. If he doesn't, that can be a giant problem, unless you plan to get rid of everybody you currently associate with and start over. You and Dick against the world? Yes, but dropping your friends like hot potatoes shouldn't be required for that type of bond to exist.

There are lots of challenges that can make it difficult to move past the initial three months of dating into a more committed relationship. Rivaling statuses, cultural differences, huge education disparities, economic gaps, religious distinctions, mutually exclusive goals...everything down to whether or not you like jelly with your peanut butter can cause long term woes if you or he feels like an outsider within both your norms. If there is no way for the two of you to bridge these divides, staying together will become uncomfortable and nearly impossible without enormous struggle and many arguments.

If you are too far apart in your general thinking, realities of life, backgrounds or where you are headed, my suggestion would be to consider friend-zoning each other. Reality speaks, it is just too damn hard to make things work. And the longer you remain a couple, the more things you need to make work. It's much easier, more peaceful, and happier when you are of like mind overall, even though you might have variations here and there. When what you view life as being has no resemblance to his view, building one together that will suit both of you in the way you each deserve is a tough nut to crack. You're more likely to become nuts in the process.

Believe me when I tell you, as time goes by, you realize just how attached you are to certain aspects of your life that you won't feel right giving up. We become fully aware of what comprises our identity through circumstances such as these. It is normal to cling to some absolutes while bargaining away others that are less meaningful in order to meld two lives together, but when the majority of what makes you and your world up does not work for the other person, you will eventually resent making the required sacrifices or taking on the necessary burdens to remain cohesively together, I promise you. This is especially true when money and finances factor into the mix.

If Jane's and Dick's views vary significantly with regards to how money is spent, saved, or managed overall, or if each of their financial aspirations don't align, in addition to their being other dramatic differences in their lifestyles, I really would recommend wishing each other good luck and goodbye. Money-based quarrels are one of the leading reasons marriages break up. And although we would like to believe that love can conquer all, most couples toss love out the window when they can't pay their bills or if one is out working his or her ass off and the other is home spending his or her heart out. Even if that is not occurring and both are working hard, money problems can still destroy a marriage.

Ultimately, your lives need to meld on most of the major levels to succeed. The beauty of the first three months of dating is that you can explore these answers and decide if it is even worth considering moving beyond this point (or the next day for that matter) with your Dick. Requesting input from your family and friends after they have had the opportunity to meet him is absolutely pertinent to your assessment of who your Dick is and how he fits into your social circle, your life, and your possible future together.

It is never too early to flush these things out, I assure you. We all have our deal-breakers, and it is better to address and be honest about yours and his *upfront* than learn that you will be forced to give up Christmas the minute you say "I do" for religious reasons or may someday be expected to move to the country to help raise cattle when the only country living you've ever seen is the image on the back of your all-natural vegan burger box.

Yup, those are the things you need to know before you fully fall in love. Find a partner, not a pain, to hold the other end of your jump rope. Otherwise, you may just find yourself considering other uses for it when you can no longer bear the thought of making one more concession.

CHAPTER 29
DICK'S FAVORITE SHIRT

Never, ever, ever date a guy thinking that you are going to improve him. Women do this all the time. They start out thinking, "This man is perfect." Eventually, however, they notice certain areas where Dick looks limp, igniting a frenzied overhaul led by Jane. Her goal is to "make his life better." His is to merely survive while somehow hanging onto his favorite shirt—you know, the one he wears over and over without ever washing it.

Yup, no matter what age men are, each has a favorite shirt and you are fooling yourself, Jane, if you think your Dick will ever outgrow it or give it up. This reality is the reason I always suggest that you spend the first three months of dating figuring out if you can actually live with that damn thing and everything else it represents.

What do I mean, exactly? I mean that what you see is what you get when it comes to a man. You can expect only a certain amount of improvement without altering your Dick to be someone he is not, and that ain't gonna happen, I assure you.

For instance, if your Dick is not a romantic today, don't expect him to pick you flowers tomorrow and present them to you in surprise fashion. If he isn't an ambitious soul, don't expect him to go out and land a paper route just because it suits your ideal. If he tends to have a sour personality, don't expect to add sugar and mix. Even if he does adopt a sweeter demeanor, it will be short-lived.

We all arrive to this earth as individuals, and you need to like the one you initially met, as that is the Dick who will be sticking around. Even if you get rid of his favorite shirt, he will still be the one staring you in the face day in and day out, unless, of course, you toss it out with him still in it.

You really need to understand the man you are embracing before you commit to anything beyond just dating him. This includes the *upside* and the *downside* of his particular personality. Finding out that he isn't anything you expected him to be after three kids and ten years behind you is not an optimum situation for anyone. So look beyond the rose-colored glasses and recognize your Dick for the man he truly is—super or "super for someone else."

I know many women who married their Dicks only to spend 19 out of 24 hours daily alone with their children. They barely see their husbands but have wads of cash to spend. They travel to the best places, wear the finest clothes, and enjoy the swankiest homes and automobiles, only to eventually tire of it all and jump into bed with Junior's camp counselor. These women loved the idea and the benefits of dating and marrying a workaholic, but they didn't realize the cost of doing so.

Alternately, I also know women who balked at the notion of marrying a man who had a solid future ahead of him as opposed to one whose artistic pursuits made them swoon. Their children are in daycare 24-7; they, themselves, are always tired from juggling work-life demands as the primary breadwinner and family caretaker; but *he* still plays a mean piano.

I realize these are two very extreme examples, but they are real and necessary to help you realize how life could unfold if you don't clean up any disillusionment you may have regarding who your Dick actually is. That said, just as his favorite shirt should appeal to you, no matter how many times he wears it, yours should appeal to him too, which means making sure that you don't pretend to be someone you are not purely to entice him into your closet.

Feeling good in your own skin should be all you need to attract Dick your way. If that does not work for him, let him walk on by. You guys are not meant to be. This isn't to say that he's wrong or you are wrong. It simply means "different strokes for different folks," and those folks need to find each other.

Personally, if the Dick I was dating suddenly asked me to stop jogging every morning because he hated my muscular legs, I'd begin to reevaluate my relationship with him. Or if he told me that I needed to reprioritize my children or my work life according to his tastes, I'd probably accommodate him but not in the way he, most likely, imagined. Those changes are just not me, and I'm not of the mind to make them.

This type of confidence, however, arises from years of living and learning. If you are not there yet or are fairly new to dating, take my advice: Make sure he shows you his and you show him yours at the beginning of the playdate. Neither of you wants to be surprised by what's hiding underneath each other's favorite shirts when it's all too late.

CHAPTER 30
DICK UNMASKED

Make sure that the Dick you are involved with is actually the same guy when he is out from under you. The last thing you need to find out, when you are on your way to being hopelessly in love, is that the man you think your Dick is, *isn't,* when he's not around you. This does occur, and you need to be aware of it.

Being proud of the person you are with is imperative to building a strong foundation for a more serious relationship. Both of you need to be honest about who you are together and who you are apart. Hopefully, they are one and the same but this may not always be the case. That is why glimpses into his life that happen to come your way when your man is doing his own thing are gifts to be pondered. Understanding the standards your Dick holds himself to on his own time can help to confirm or hinder your feelings for him as well as the trust you've placed in him and the judgment you've used in agreeing to date him. It's part of the full-disclosure aspect of your budding relationship that he can't provide but others can.

For instance, if your friend happens to see your man pay for an ice cream cone for a little boy (short on pennies) whom he met in the line at Dairy Queen, and she lets you in on it, that's valuable information to have. The same would hold true if, alternately, he shoved the boy to the side the minute the entire line found out the kid didn't have enough money, leaving him coneless while he, himself, ordered up a hot-fudge sundae. Certainly, upon finding this out, you'd have a lot of questions floating around in your head. I know I would.

Every woman wants to know who she is dealing with and, ultimately, sleeping with when dating, and one side of this is knowing what your Dick does when he is outside of your range of observation. As much as he will tell you about himself, you can learn a ton more from unexpected instances like these, as well as through stories from others who know him today and have known him for years.

However the disclosure comes, grab it, think it through, then file it in the folder that you are keeping, the one which will help you to determine whether or not you will begin month number four as his official girlfriend. That said, realize that you won't know everything about him in the first three months of dating. We all have years of living we bring into every relationship and, as much as I believe in full disclosure between dating individuals, especially of all of the monumental experiences that have shaped you in your life, I do suggest applying common sense to the timing of certain disclosures that may be a bit more difficult to explain—the ones that might just send either Dick or you packing.

For instance, I once agreed to have dinner with a gentleman who told me a very unnerving story, the details of which caused me enormous concern. Now successful, he attributed the origins of his success to a time in his life when he was so poor that he had to eat his own fishing bait to survive. Poor fishing skills combined with unfortunate circumstances left him down and out as well as hungry. He would eventually turn his life around and, at the time of our dinner, owned a thriving business. He also seemed relatively happy.

It was quite a story to hear on a first date, and although I respected this gentleman's determination, resourcefulness, and fortitude, the images of him eating his own bait and living in the swamps with the alligators (it gets worse, I kid you not) could not be wiped clean. Even so, I did my best to listen without judgment. I then thanked him for dinner and went my separate way. It ultimately worked out for the best, I tell you, but I have found myself occasionally wondering what would have happened had he told me that very same story a few months later, after I had gotten to know him better. I could only guess that my shock would have been more manageable and my decision to see or not see him again, less hasty. Timing is everything in life and in dating.

Although I do believe that it is critical to divulge just about everything to your partner in a committed relationship, I also think you can hold back a bit while dating, just until you feel comfortable sharing, and that is only if what you are holding back has no real consequence or impact on your time together currently. In other words, if your night job is the headlining stripper at a local bar, I'd suggest letting him know before he finds out on his own. That type of surprise never ends well and will, most likely, mean the end of your time together if you choose to hold back this revelation until a later date.

Whereas honesty is the best policy, Jane, knowing when it is the right time to open a can of worms can be the difference between enjoying each other's company and wishing you had eaten your words instead.

Relationship

You're just great,
He did relate,
Over coffee,
On their first date.

So are you,
That'd make two,
Three years later,
They'd say, "I do."

CHAPTER 31

SEE JANE RUN

Speaking of first dates, there is certain protocol that you should follow when out with your Dick for the first time and for several times thereafter. Obviously, the more you get to know this guy, the more rule-bending you can expect to do, but some things you should never allow to happen—like farting in front of him without trying to exhibit a modicum of restraint. That goes for him too, by the way, although men seem to fart much more liberally than women.

In any event, my number one rule of thumb is to keep safety at the forefront of your mind during the initial stage of dating (and every other stage, but definitely this one). This means that, although he may be an absolute gentleman in offering to pick you up your first time out together, kindly say thank you but drive yourself. The last thing you want to do is to be subject to his will, either at the place where you plan to meet or while traveling between your home and there. Until you know him better, don't get into his car with him. Common sense will let you know when all's clear, I assure you. Only then should you give him your address and invite him to take this baby step forward. He will respect you for it and realize that he needs to prove himself to you before he gets keys of any kind (this includes to your heart).

Another rule I have that makes quite a good deal of sense is, unless you've already met once in person, get together in a setting that does not include alcohol. Not what you want to hear, I know but there is a valid reason for this. Simply put, most guys look good after a glass of wine or a mixed drink. You need to be able to qualify the Dick sitting in front of you without alcohol running through your bloodstream so that you know whether or not he's worth giving another try. Being tipsy won't help you do this. Find a place for coffee or meet for a walk (in a busy park)...anything but at a bar or similar joint.

I also believe that it is quite alright if you agree to eat a meal with him on the first date. If he is willing to stick it out, you should be too. And honestly, even if you and Dick are not a romantic match, Jane, you can certainly still appreciate a congenial exchange with another human being. Sometimes you can make some pretty good friends this way. That said, if he turns out to be a real dud, understand that you can excuse yourself at any point and leave. I would recommend this in those unexpected cases such as when he looks nothing like his photo, insults you or tells you that he ate his mother for breakfast that very same morning.

Don't pay the check or agree to pay the check. We covered this and the many reasons why in an earlier chapter, so I need not go over it again here. Just **don't** do it!

Be kind and well-mannered, as this experience is as nerve-wracking for him as it is for you. Keep that in mind and help carry the conversation along. I also suggest that you dedicate at least an hour to the date going into it as some people need a 'warm up period' to get comfortable and show their true colors. If after that, it's really not working, be honest and gently say so. Most men would prefer to know this upfront than wait around for a return phone call they ain't gonna get.

If you are able to, keep first dates to the daytime, when you can see him clearly. Evening dates influence feelings and inspire romance where there may be none otherwise. Plus, it is much tougher not to drink in the moonlight. If, however, you do get together at night and do order a drink, and he doesn't, do not hesitate to ask him why he chose not to. There are all sorts of reasons people don't drink. Give him the space to explain his and know that his choice may very well impact your life down the road. It's good information to have initially, especially for all of you who like squashed grapes and hops regularly. If he invites you to join him for a glass of wine on a private beach somewhere, acknowledge the lovely notion, but suggest saving it for when you know him better.

As your first date comes to a close, properly thanking him provides the perfect opportunity to clearly indicate whether or not you want to see him again. This is where both grace and finesse come into play. If you like him, giving him a quick hug while telling him that you had a wonderful time should open the door to his suggesting another outing. If it doesn't, don't push the matter. He will let you know his true feelings and intentions soon enough.

If you can't stand him, don't lead him on. Allow your body language to tell the tale as graciously as possible. Merely stand back from him while saying goodbye and wish him well. If he goes in for a smooch, only then can you punch him in the face. Only kidding! Violence is never the answer, especially if he did eat his mother that morning. Angering him will surely place you next on his menu.

If you are on the fence about him, I suggest not immediately shutting down another opportunity to get together. I myself have found that it sometimes takes me two meetings to ascertain whether or not I like a guy. I need the familiarity of the second meeting to help me decide, unless there is such an obviousness about the Dick that nothing further need be revealed. In that case, I either do or I don't.

If at the end of your first date you each conclude that you had a great time, exchange the necessary contact information beyond what you already have, and ask him to text you when he arrives home. Men love when women do this, because it shows them that we care about their well-being. This doesn't give you permission, however, to assume that you are already involved in a relationship with Dick or he you. Keep his trust sacred (as well as his contact information) and don't hound him with it. Hounding him will surely change your nice time together into a "dog" and you too. Give him space to breathe and chase you down. The more you do this, the more he will be a-chasin', I assure you.

At this point, you need to keep your eyes open to stay aware of any form of game-playing he may begin to do. Some Dicks love the chase and then lose interest once you indicate any form of interest in them whatsoever. If you are at the stage in life where game-playing isn't for you, don't participate. He will get the message and be forced to make a decision. If you are happy to play his game because you, Jane, aren't ready to settle down either, so be it.

To that end, if he takes longer than a day after your date to text or email you a quick follow-up message indicating his enjoyment of your company and desire to see you again, expect to play some games with this Dick as the guy isn't fully onboard. If he wants you, he will be falling all over himself for a second date even if he appears to be "cool as a cucumber" in the process.

Also, decide what message you want to send him through the clothes you wear. It is fine to show a little skin but inviting his eyeballs to jump down your shirt will only hinder his ability to get to know the rest of you. It's not what our evolved ears want to hear but it's accurate, nonetheless. So don't do that. You are much more than the body you are in. Project this, as that is what will truly make you attractive to him, long term. This isn't to say to arrive to the date looking like a slob or a Puritan. Let's be realistic. Men are visual creatures. Wear clothes that you feel good in—that increase your ease and enjoyment of the date. *Class* and *comfort* are terrific standards of measure when choosing your outfit. You can't go wrong with either, and they will help him see you and your time together for what you want it to be.

That said, notice how he dresses too along with his overall posture, ability to communicate, manners, and any annoying habits that immediately jump out at you and hold your eyeballs hostage. Don't be overly critical, but at the same time, respect what Sally has to say when all three of you are sitting together and react accordingly. She won't lead you astray even if you are trying to convince yourself that this guy is perfect for you because you are tired of being alone and searching for that right Dick has all but done you in.

No one ever told you that dating would be easy, but neither is living your life with the wrong Dick. In fact, that is a lot harder, I assure you. Opt to put the time and effort into finding the right Dick now so that you needn't repeat the process or regret not having done so. Finding the right man will only get tougher with age, believe you me.

Another rule to commit to: Don't kiss him! This does not mean that you can't give him a quick peck on the cheek at the end of your first date if you truly like him and appreciate the time you spent together. That makes for a wonderful opening for him to swoop on in and ask you out again. But don't open-mouth him for any reason. If you see his tongue heading your way, assume he is going to eat your face and stop him. Frankly, that's sorta disgusting and truly disrespectful. It is also a strong indication that his tongue wanders around town frequently, and if it does, I'd question what other part on this Dick does too.

Speaking of which, definitely don't sleep with him on the first date no matter how attractive he is or electric you are together. You can't retract that step once you take it. And even if he sees you again after that, sex will become the priority for him with you as opposed to getting to know the incredible being you are. Save this type of intimacy for later when there is more than just physical pleasure involved.

Now if you do happen to know the Dick you are going out with and have met him face-to-face prior to your date, allowing him to pick you up is perfectly fine so long as you are comfortable. For instance, if he works at the same company you do, I don't see why you can't hop in the car with him to grab lunch somewhere. Or if he sits in the same college class as you and would like to whisk you off to grab two iced lattes, you needn't hesitate to agree. Those situations make complete sense, and your familiarity with this Dick provides you a reasonable amount of assurance that he's not looking to suck on your bones unless you are alive and breathing. Certainly, consult with Sally on the matter but if all feels fine, go for it, which does not mean throw caution to the wind or lose your wits. It means, get into his car with both eyes open and figure out what you would do if, in fact, you needed to get out quickly or fight your way out.

Now, if the Dick you happen to be meeting for a first date is your best friend, having suddenly morphed into a romantic interest, getting into his car is a no brainer, unlike the realities that come with dating your best friend. There are true benefits to this kind of relationship. His being your best friend is a wonderful beginning point for a more committed and deeper relationship to unfold. He knows you and you obviously know him. Now, he wants you. Tale told. That said, if something goes awry, such as he begins to wrestle with a bit of confusion as to what he really wants after all, the situation can become messy and negatively impact the stellar friendship the two of you have. "Tread lightly and slowly" is the wisest piece of advice that I can give. And again, ask Sally.

Finally, don't place too much pressure on your first date. If the sky doesn't open up and launch a rainbow by the end of it, that's OK. The right Dick will come along. If this Dick isn't the one, another will follow. Don't lose heart. If he possibly could be the one but you need more time to decide, revel in the notion that you met a promising prospect and enjoy getting to know him. If, however, a rainbow is in clear sight and prodding you to ride it, bask in the excitement of having this new man in your life and keep any *riding* to the rainbow, itself, for a while, at least until you learn whether or not the pot of gold located at the end of it is worth the one sitting in front of him.

CHAPTER 32

JANE PLAYS PRETEND

These days, it is as natural to be on a dating website when single as dating itself (or even when *not* single, unfortunately, but that's a whole other book and issue). Dating websites have exploded and serve all kinds of daters. If you want a cowboy, a farmer or some other unique bend in your Dick, there's a dating website specifically for you.

Frankly, I think they are fun, but they can also be a headache. Crafting your profile, posting it for everyone to see, and then waiting for the initial deluge of eager Dicks to subside can be both thrilling and flattering. The process of vetting the profiles of anxious suitors, however, that can begin to feel more like a second job. Then there is finally deciding upon whom to speak with and possibly meet. By this time, you may find yourself nearly tapped out of any available hours left in your schedule, only to be left feeling upset, alone, and lonely once again. Sound familiar?

There is no perfect science to the entire ordeal, despite promotional claims to the contrary. I recommend you consider dating websites to be just another available dating route to travel down and don't think much more into them...unless, of course, you are the nearly naked gal who feels that this particular photo is the optimal one to post. You, my dear, need to do a great deal more thinking, then change the photo that is spreading a negative cast over all of us Janes as a result of your own poor judgment.

When it comes to dating websites, women should live by the golden rule that less is more. Less skin, less personal information, and less obsessing. Talk but don't stalk and guard your privacy as much as possible. It's tough in this social media age to do this, but you need to, as you never know who is on the other side of that screen. Dating websites can be dangerous.

Keep kids off the grid and out of all photos too. "Plain Jane" it, Jane, so that you live to regret nothing. And follow the rules already set forth in prior chapters. Yes, these sites are host to many wonderful men who are searching for exactly what you are, but they are also home to a ton of liars, predators, and thieves. Don't be naive, overly eager or stupid in your search. This is not just your happiness but your safety, life, and future we are talking about, as well as your children's if you have them.

I also suggest waiting to be pursued online, just as I do in-person. Allow Dick to come to you, although you can open the door with a wink or by adding him to your "favorites" and see if he moseys your way as a result. But don't outright send him a come-hither message. It's not smart or necessary. If he wants you, he will think up a clever message of his own to prod your interest and interaction.

And for heaven's sake, don't use dating websites as hook-up sites. God knows what you could pick up even when practicing "safe sex," which you should *always* do. I can't stress this enough. You could also be taking your life into your hands, which would have devastating consequences for more than just you. The impact on your loved ones, if anything should happen to you, would be very real. Don't be reckless, Jane.

Finally, be honest in your profile, including with your photos, and hold him accountable as well. If you or he arrives to your first date looking nothing like your pictures or professing lifestyles or occupations that neither of you have, that places you both in the category of "liar," and there is nowhere to go from there. You are much more likely to attract the guy you actually want by being who you actually are.

Birds of a feather flock together, Jane, and the last position you want to find yourself in is the one that places you at the center of his rage for not being completely truthful with him when you had the chance to be. Same goes for him. No one wants a partner who they can't trust or who isn't proud enough of who she or he is to share it willingly.

As I said, dating websites can be fun and can bring you one step closer to finding the partner you've been looking for, but they can also be tricky and become a bane in your existence. Keep conscious of what you are doing when you are on them. Know when it is time to get off them. And spend as little time obsessing over your overall results as possible.

They are not foolproof. Proceed with caution and appreciate dating websites for what they can offer. They are a great alternative to meeting the old-fashioned way, which, although better in my opinion, is becoming much harder to do in the world we currently live in.

One final note: Men who don't post photos have their reasons. Be suspicious. Men who ask you to lend them money through these sites are con artists. Unless you are a private investigator or an educated banker, I recommend that you back away from both. No doubt, you will be giving up some riveting stories in the process, but the library is always open at school and who knows? You might just find your right Dick sitting there instead.

CHAPTER 33

JANE LOVES HER DOLLY

Having mentioned kids in the previous chapter, I wanted to take this opportunity to jump right into that topic, as I have very strong feelings on the matter. Here's where I stand on children and dating. As a responsible mother, you must never allow a man you are dating to take a front seat to your children. Furthermore, dump the man who insists otherwise. Children *always* come first, and any Dick worth your time will want this too.

Children are a blessing, pure and simple. This doesn't mean that they can't be "trying" at times or won't muddy up your dating plans now and again; but once you have them, you are a package deal, and there are plenty of men out there anxiously looking for that package. You might be surprised by how many men missed the boat on having kids despite the fact that they had truly wanted them. Finding a woman with a ready-made family fills that empty spot in their lives, allowing them to revel in being stepdads while expanding and supporting the children's and your world in all kinds of valuable ways.

If both of you have children, consider the coupling twice as much fun but also twice as much work in scheduling dates and getting to know each other. Even so, if you truly want to, you will figure it out, and if all goes well, in time, you will be able to include the children in your plans. I suggest taking the last step slowly, though. Rushing could backfire on the two of you in ways you just can't anticipate.

That said, children do possess the unique ability to help flush out the good Dicks from the bad ones, as they tend to be naturally empathic. Don't overlook their ability to read your Dick better than you from the start. If they show any reticence in greeting him and share their concerns with you once he drops you at the door, consider their feelings seriously, as you may be missing something. Remember, your children are on your side. As you are the most important person in their lives, they want to protect you as much as you do them. That said, keep in mind that they are still children and you must maintain the final say in your dating life.

Personally, I don't believe that there really is a perfect time to introduce your children to your date, as there are studies that substantiate both sides of that argument—*sooner* or *later*. You know your kids best, ultimately. I think if you maintain a strong connection with them, address any insecurities that come up as a result of your dating, and continue to parent in a responsible manner, you place everyone involved on the best possible footing.

That doesn't mean, though, that you have a license to invite every Tom, Dick, or Harry home to meet the young 'uns or leave any of these gentlemen alone with the kids for even a second until much further down the line. You can never be too cautious when it comes to your children. It does mean, however, to use common sense in making each judgment call according to the situation and circumstances at hand. For instance, if you need to pick up your son at baseball practice and your date happens to be sitting next to you in the car after a shared cup of coffee, swinging by the field to collect your son, then nicely introducing the two of them is a convenient and easy way to make an introduction.

How your son reacts will depend upon a lot of things, many more than can be covered in this chapter. Hopefully, the moment proves to be a simple one, but even if it doesn't, don't kick yourself. Expect to make a ton of mistakes while dating, and this includes where your kids are involved.

Just do your best. Don't expect perfection. And realize that finding the right Dick will benefit your children too. One of the best gifts you can give your kids is the opportunity to see a loving relationship between two adults...especially if one of them is their mother.

You have to start somewhere, Jane. And the words "I'm sorry" can mend a lot of fences with your kids. It can also offer them the opportunity to learn how to comfortably say it to others throughout their own lives. And just imagine if you get it right...how happy might you all be? Everything can be turned into a lesson, Jane, if you want it to be—even dating blunders. Don't forget that. Just don't abuse it either.

CHAPTER 34

JANE GROWS UP

Dating when you are age 40 and over is a much different experience than when you are in your 20s and 30s. Men perceive you in a whole new way. You arrive with a maturity, wisdom, and comfort in yourself that younger women just don't have. And all of this shows up in your face, your skin, and in every other part of you—freaking some of you out while calming others.

The fact is, you can't turn back the clock, Jane, and trying to as an older woman will last for only so long. Eventually, your years will catch up with you, no matter how much cream you rub on your face or plastic surgery you elect to do. I view it as immensely unfortunate that we Janes have made such an enemy of time, when time truly is our best friend. We only get better with it and, although I admire the beauty of young women in their 20s and 30s, I would not want to trade the age I am today for one less line in my forehead or at the corners of my mouth. I earned them and am damn proud of all that went into the creation of every one of them.

It disheartens me when I see older women try to be something they are not. They've bought into the idea that to be beautiful, you have to be young. It is my belief that to be beautiful, you have to be you. Beauty comes in all types of packages, and if you have the chance to travel, it will dispel any myths you may have to the contrary.

What makes a woman beautiful is subjective in nature. We live according to the standards of the countries we are from, but that does not necessarily make them right or right for you. I've seen women whose faces, body types, and ages fail to meet the measures of beauty common to the United States, and yet they were incredibly attractive, engaging, intelligent, and vibrant women.

Personally, I find myself, at age fifty-one, to be in the best shape and place I've ever been. I keep myself fit through exercise and eat as healthy a diet as possible, although not perfect by any means. I seek out growth, enjoyment, and adventure at every turn and have learned to prioritize my life and minimize my stress (or at least handle it better than when I was younger). My face, well...it boasts higher cheekbones today and is a bit more pointed than in photos of my past, but these are the features of my ancestors, and I am enormously proud of those people, so why wouldn't I be proud of what they left me, which includes the *dignity* and *self-respect* that come along with knowing better?

It is unfortunate how rare those two characteristics have become today, especially in dating. They are two of the most attractive attributes a woman (of any age) can have, and yet they currently seem to be missing in one too many aging and dating Janes, which is negatively impacting their success in finding the right Dicks for them.

I believe that if you don't claim dignity and self-respect for yourself, you won't project them. Nor will you get them from Dick. You are not fooling anyone by dressing like your teenage daughter for a dinner date. You are saying a ton about yourself as well as how you feel about our gender as a whole. I know I don't appreciate that for myself, my young daughters or any other woman. It's the type of thinking that reinforces harmful stereotypes.

Additionally, Dicks who are attracted to women who demonstrate such insecurities are not worth your time. There are plenty of men of all ages who seek out older women to date simply because they like and want what a woman who has a few years under her belt brings to the table. Robbing the cradle ain't where these men are at. They want the companionship, friendship, relationship, and even sex that older women offer.

Don't shun aging for any reason, including dating. Embrace it, Jane! There is a lot more to look forward to when you do than any result that might come from whatever your plastic surgeon can cut and paste together...including your eyes, which for many single older Janes are now sitting directly on the sides of their heads as a result of one too many plastic surgeries. I promise you, there isn't a Dick in the world who is looking for a flounder for a girlfriend or a wife no matter what her age!

CHAPTER 35

DICK GROWS UP

How old a man is will definitely impact the date that you have with him, Jane. There is no getting around this. Obviously, the closer you are in age, the more likely you are to share pertinent commonalities despite varying life experiences. At the same time, however, that does not guarantee success by any means.

There are pros and cons to dating men older and younger than you, and you should weigh them all before settling on an agreeable age range for yourself when choosing men to date. There are wonderful, mature, interesting, attractive, and exciting Dicks of all ages looking for like women to take out and get to know. There are also realities to every one of them, including if you date either way below or way above your own age.

We've all seen winter–spring romances blossom and some work out very well, but others end up with spring becoming the youthful caretaker of winter. Where once a distinguished gentleman sat, now sits an old man needing a lot of help to walk up and down the stairs. Becoming dependent on our partners and loved ones happens to all of us, but inviting the strain of that responsibility so early on in your years can be incredibly limiting and stressful. It takes great care not to become resentful of your partner when he can't keep up with you despite how meaningful he has been throughout your life together. That's just reality speaking, folks.

At the same time, dating someone your own age or younger poses different obstacles. For instance, many women find younger men to be physically appealing but considerably less mature. This is not always the case, but I've heard many Janes complain about it and I've experienced it myself.

Since women usually outlive men, dating a younger man offers a certain sense of security that you may not end up living the back end of your life alone, but this may not always hold true. My late husband and I were five years apart, and I lost him to cancer when I was 35 years-old. Death doesn't discriminate according to age and you can only prepare for and prevent so much.

I think ultimately you need to ascertain the reasons you are dating in order to fit the right Dick into the open slot that is your life. If you are looking for a long term partner, the person you choose will be quite different than if you are looking for a Dick to hang around with for now. Age matters less in the latter case and a great deal more in the former.

Additionally, and even more important in my opinion simply because time is such a valuable commodity, you should choose a man who makes your life better for having him in it. Seems obvious but you'd be surprised. Given you do this, however, I'm not quite sure how you could go wrong outside of life's total uncertainty.

Just do your best to make the right choice for you, then hold your nose and jump. You will fall somewhere, I assure you. And in this case, hopefully, it is *in love*.

CHAPTER 36

DICK MINDS HIS PS AND QS

In the first three months of dating, Dick may seem to fill every gap you have in your life. But sooner or later, you are going to come to realize that your Dick can fill only so many gaps. He will fall short—not because he wants to but because he is human.

The reality is that no one person can complete us. Family, friends, coworkers, acquaintances, the Uber driver who just dropped you off at your hair appointment downtown...they all add something to your life that helps to make you feel whole. To expect Dick to accomplish such a monumental task all by himself is unrealistic and unfair. Only in the movies can such delusions truly exist.

That said, I do believe that your Dick bears more responsibility for your overall happiness, contentment, and wholeness than, let's say, your dry cleaner (although a really good dry cleaner has been known to make women break out in song, I assure you), a responsibility that only increases as the seriousness of his relationship with you does. The more "in" your Dick is with you, the more Ps and Qs he needs to mind. "What does she mean by this?" you ask. Allow me to explain.

There are five non-negotiable Ps that every man is obligated to live up to in a marital relationship so that the Brothers Q—Quiver and Quake—don't come knocking on the door of your shared treehouse. Those Ps are Provide, Protect, Play, Push, and Persevere. If your Dick minds those Ps, he will surely be demonstrating your importance to him as well as his commitment to your overall welfare and your marriage. Therefore, knowing where he stands on these upfront is just good planning, Jane. It will prevent you from climbing the wrong tree and getting stuck.

I doubt there is any confusion posed by the first P—Provide. Your Dick needs to be able to provide for you, financially and otherwise, even if you too are providing. Bills are real and not being able to pay them is just as good as extending an open invitation to the Brothers Q to come live with you and destroy your marriage.

The second P—Protect—should also be fairly self-explanatory. Your Dick needs to want to protect you from scary creatures that go bump in the night and everything else that sends you careening into his arms for safety's sake.

The third P—Play—seems obvious as well. He needs to be able to add to the fun that makes each of you the other's biggest fan and more devoted to each other every day.

The fourth P—Push—may not be apparent at all. Your Dick needs to be able to push you to be the best that you can be and help you to grow throughout your entire life.

The final P—Perseverance—might also be a little tricky. Your Dick needs to demonstrate his dedication to you and your marriage through thick and thin.

If you meet a guy who is looking to mind these Ps in order to give the woman he eventually marries the support and security she needs while deterring the Brothers Q from beating both your asses along the way, date him. This Dick has the makings of a great date and an even better long term relationship.

My advice to you would be to jump on him before another Jane does. No, he still won't be the only one you need to complete you but realizing that he will do everything in his power to help you achieve this makes this Dick a real-life superhero and as close to movie-perfect as you are ever going to get.

By minding his own Ps and Qs, he's looking after yours too, Jane. He's a keeper for certain and someone you really need to devote some time to getting to know. You won't regret it.

<u>Romance</u>

To begin,
She walked in.
To the end,
He would spend...
Loving her.

CHAPTER 37
JANE'S FAVORITE LETTER

When it comes to dating, the letter "S" is Jane's best friend. It might be hard to accept for some women but most Dicks want a *soft, steady,* and *strong* Jane to spend time with and potentially marry. A woman who exhibits this combination will ignite a sense of confidence that will allow Dick to go out into the world and conquer it for the two of them.

Years ago, they used to school women in art and culture while emphasizing beauty and social graces that she could bring into the home. They did this because they saw value in such refinement, ensuring that a woman would remain "soft" in the masculine world she was living in. I'm not advocating that we return to these days, by any means, but I do believe that having a soft side as a woman is a trait that appeals to men rather significantly.

It's tough out there, more so than ever before. Men like to know that they can come home to a woman who understands and will help to soften the daily blows he must endure in making a living, even if she is adding to the pot too. That may sound archaic and really hard to hear, but liking reality and accepting reality can be two very different things. At no time is this more evident than today.

Additionally, men are also highly visual creatures, who are attracted to feminine attributes, as they were designed this way. The softer, more curvaceous features of Jane make him happy. Again, you can try to argue this truth based on all kinds of studies, but the best test is to merely ask the average man what he looks for in a woman. Part of his answer will most surely include the attractiveness of Jane's physical appearance. Numerous cosmetic and fashion companies bank on that fact.

Another characteristic Dicks look for in Janes is "steadiness." A man doesn't want a roller coaster for a life, so he doesn't want a roller coaster for a wife. When he dates you, he wants to know that he can rely on you to be there to smooth out the tough times that might lie ahead if, in fact, you guys end up doing more than just dating. He needs to find a partner all the way. And although it can be extremely exciting to date a woman who rises and falls on a whim, marrying her tends to be a risky bet for a man who is actually seriously interested in settling down.

The final of the three characteristics that Dick is looking for has nothing to with physical appearance or any muscle power whatsoever. "Strong" in this sense of the word refers to *emotional* and *intellectual* strength. Dick wants to know that the Jane he is dating can excel where he falls short as well as counsel him effectively. He wants to know that the children they have together—if they choose to have kids—will benefit from both sides of the family tree, ultimately producing people better than themselves, especially if he ends up being absent from home more regularly than she.

Finding all three characteristics in one Jane can make Dick behave in ways quite unlike himself normally. So concerned with the competition from other potential suitors, Dicks have been known to dance about wildly (so to speak) to block Jane's view of any other possible mates just waiting to scoop her up too. The entire escapade can be rather dazzling and, at times, even overwhelming to Jane. It can also be charming, flattering and downright funny, yet another simple reminder of how unevolved we evolved humans beings actually are especially when it comes to courtship.

CHAPTER 38

DICK AND JANE
TRADE COMPLIMENTS

One of the most wonderful parts of dating during the first three months is that the two of you feel so special. Your world sorta shrinks to just him and you. You become each other's center, and you focus on doing both little and big things that bring each other immeasurable joy.

He buys you flowers. You text him a note letting him know that you think he is an incredible man. He calls you just to hear your voice. You send him a song you absolutely need to share. These are the heartfelt gestures of which romance and relationships are made of, and they couldn't be more important.

So why do we stop?

Compliments and signs of affection are imperative to building and keeping alive closeness between a man and a woman. Each of us needs those little reminders to make us feel appreciated as well as grateful that the person we've always wanted, the guy or girl who truly "sees" us, is finally here and wants to be part of our life, facades off! Tokens of affection are important and you should never give them up, no matter how many years you spend in each other's company.

The very first time you show how meaningful he is to you through a gift or act, you set the stage for similar thoughtfulness. Even simple tasks, like him bringing you lunch on a busy day, should not go unnoticed or unmentioned. Thanking him for thinking of you will ensure that "lunch" is not a singular occurrence but part of his continuous caring for you. Just as you baking him his favorite cookies and packing him up a bagful of them as he walks out the door will go a long way as well. To a man, these types of kindnesses speak volumes. No man can pass up a cookie, I assure you. Seems old-fashioned but men like baked goods and receiving them from a woman is a big deal, even today. "The way to a man's heart is through his stomach" still rings true.

Every time you make a man feel special—you praise him for accomplishments, efforts or just plain thoughtfulness, Jane—you empower him to do the same and keep the relationship and *you* first. If what you do results in anything else, you two are not meant to be. Same goes for you in the reverse, by the way.

Unfortunately for many couples, when life eventually moves them back to a place where they must, now, include more people in their perfectly adjoined world, too many times those little acts of adoration, appreciation, and applause get tossed over the fence. I advise you to not be one of those couples.

When you find a great guy who is into you too, and he gifts you with a token of affection, make sure you return the favor by expressing how much his thoughtfulness means to you. And meet his kindness with a gesture of your own.

Certain things we don't forget, like the first time you received a carnation at school on Valentine's Day. Or the moment your Dick told you that you were the most beautiful woman he ever saw. Or the day a silver butterfly charm on a chain became the beginning of the two of you catching them together for the rest of your lives. All these acts are extraordinarily meaningful, symbols of intimacy, affection, and love. They need to be cherished.

Never lose this between you and never not do them. Remember the thrill of trading baseball cards on the blacktop and winning? That's what you will feel like, and even better, if you trade compliments and more with your Dick for however long your relationship lasts. The only difference is that the two of you will walk away winners.

Making someone feel special takes very little time and lots of 'wanting to'. So if it does not seem appealing to you with the Dick you are dating or if he isn't showing any signs of eagerness, himself, take a second look at the blacktop and see who's waiting there, patiently, to trade. You will undoubtedly attract another Dick soon. And once you do, remember to keep your cards turned down at all times, for the moment anyway. He will let you know whether or not you should turn them right side up, I assure you. Dicks always do, one way or another.

CHAPTER 39

JANE TELLS TIME

Dating takes time and so does Dick. Those are two facts that you need to be fully aware of prior to wandering down this road. If you are not able to devote the proper time it takes to date and find the right Dick, it's better to 'opt out' of the process for the moment because, ultimately, you will not be happy with your results and may become put off altogether.

It isn't abnormal for Janes to be short on time even if they are long on desire to find their perfect match. We live extremely busy lives today. Taking a break from dating because we've spread ourselves too thin or have tired from the ritual after many months of disappointing results is not uncommon. You just don't feel like kissing one more frog today, and so you refrain from placing yourself next to the pond for the moment. There is nothing wrong or odd about that.

We all know how emotionally grueling and physically taxing dating can be. You need to be in the right headspace to do it. Admittedly, in my lifetime, I've taken long reprieves from the entire process for reasons that run the gamut, including getting myself to a place that I felt I needed to be to attract the type of Dick I wanted to attract. I truly believe that one of the best contributions you can make to yourself, your future, and your future Dick is to devote the time you need to craft yourself into becoming the person you've always wanted to be—a person of character, accomplishment, and whatever else you deem necessary to feel good about yourself. Once you do this, you are then ready to date.

This isn't to imply that you need to be "perfect" at everything on your list of personal requirements before you look up and smile at a Dick who is staring at you from across a crowded room. It just means that self-improvement can help you to attract the same caliber of person, because like meets like and so does love.

Additionally, the happier you are with yourself, the more this will resonate, which only makes dating that much easier. People are attracted to happy people, and men like to date happy women. You want to date a happy Dick, don't you? Same thing. Misery might make great company, but it doesn't make for great bedfellows or relationships.

As I said, dating takes time to do. You need to plan, prepare, and primp for every occasion that you leave the house in order to sift through the frogs to find that one prince. Then once you do encounter him and he's swept you off of your feet, you need to keep him interested by being actively engaged and excited by the relationship and his presence in your life. Men equate feeling special with *time spent*. If you don't make time for him or make the time to do the little things that will keep him around, he won't stick around. Would you, if the shoe were on the other foot? I think not. Glass slippers are only offered to Janes who make time for the prince. If you don't have it to give, don't become disheartened when the next woman wears this one-of-a-kind footwear down the aisle.

There is grand appreciation in being available to Dick. If he is the right guy for you, he will notice your efforts and let you know he does in ways that make you glad you waded your way through all those frogs. The muck might not have felt worth it at the time, but meeting the guy who accepts and loves you for you, finally, helps to make sense of every last slimy kiss you had to endure, doesn't it? (The English language could not have provided a better word than "slimy" to describe these experiences!)

One last thought with regards to time. Respect but do not get bogged down by the increasingly loud ticking of your biological clock. Nor should you allow it to influence your choice in Dicks. The most valuable time you can spend, if you want to get married someday and especially if you plan to have children, is the time you take to find the right partner. We all make mistakes, but if you can prevent this one by merely being more diligent, thoughtful, careful, and slower-paced before you tie the knot, you will save time in the end plus a small fortune and a tremendous amount of perennial agony given a few tadpoles come along.

CHAPTER 40

DICK SWOONS

As scientific research has noted that it only takes a few milliseconds to decide whether or not you fancy someone, falling in love at first sight may not be an illusion for Dicks and Janes after all. Personally, I believe it happens as I've felt it in my own life. Call me a hopeless romantic if you must, but I am not the only one who can make such a wild claim.

Countless couples over the ages have experienced the sudden explosion of love in their hearts when unexpectedly encountering the man or woman of their dreams. And many of those relationships have endured for the long haul. Although love was not the only reason for this, it was a key element in it alongside others, including trust, respect, dedication, and workability. As noted previously, there is a practical side to love that needs to be acknowledged in order to keep Dick and Jane on the same page in dating and over the course of a lifetime.

My advice would be to never shut down the possibility of it happening to you or any other Jane even if you happen to be more of a pessimist. I would also not overlook the possibility that soul mates actually do exist, as there are couples in the world so in tune with each other from the get go that there seems to be no other explanation, which does not discount science but sometimes actually includes and then moves beyond it.

In my opinion, unless you've experienced it yourself, you really can't know or question the validity of the sudden magic shared between two people who seem just as happy at 80 together as they were when they first met at 18. Whatever other term you might call it, call it working.

There is much more to this world than what many pragmatists would lead to you believe, but to me, true love is anything but pragmatic, which is separate and apart from the dynamics required to make a relationship work. Love is indefinable by nature. In fact, if you can define it, it's wrong. Mark my words.

CHAPTER 41

DICK AND JANE
PLAY TOGETHER

Being able to laugh and have fun with your Dick even when you are basically doing nothing together is a very good sign for the two of you and your possible future as a couple. You have to be able to enjoy each other's company even when there isn't some sort of major event happening. *Atmosphere* should naturally occur between both Dick and Jane without outside fireworks being orchestrated all the time, as normal life is not that way. It's much more mundane. With the right partner, however, the word "mundane" can be turned on its ear.

Whether you are driving together to the local mechanic to get your Dick's tire plugged or repairing a stone wall, just you and him, tasks like these epitomize real-life adventures and opportunities to spend quality time and fun time. No, neither of these routine necessities is sexy or even close to being exciting from the outside looking in, but from the inside looking out, it can be everything you need to trade smiles.

As I define "spending your life with someone" as "the eternal playdate," Janes need to look for Dicks who make them feel happy by just 'showing up.' This might sound very basic and not at all fancy, but it is true. A guy who can make you beam by merely walking in the door is a guy you want to date and consider playing house with. A guy who needs to arrive with a parade trailing behind him in order to make you feel the least bit interested is not the Dick for you. Understand the difference and acknowledge in which seat you are sitting. Parades are fine. We all like them on occasion. But if you require one to make any Dick seem more appealing, then become entranced by the tuba player puffing his heart out while marching by, I'd say you have your answer. Follow the tuba player and allow your Dick to find another Jane. It is only fair, and if you learn just one lesson from this book, I hope it is the importance of being fair when dating.

We all have feelings, and even though men present tough exteriors, their hearts can be crushed too alongside their egos. Always act from a place of kindness and consideration when letting a man know that he just isn't for you. Be human, because he is as well and just may learn from what you demonstrate how to behave towards another Jane whom he may, someday, have to let down too. Character is bred in others by exemplifying it ourselves. Dating requires character and it also invites like character into our lives.

When dating a man, always put yourself in his position and take the moral high ground in your choices and behavior for yourself as much as for him. In other words, if you like a Dick but just don't feel the earth move when your lips lock, let him know as soon as the opportunity arises. Don't drag his heart around on a string just because you are bored or because he provides you the ability to be out and about so that you might find another Dick while still in his company—this is not fair, kind or considerate. Taking the high ground goes back to maintaining a sense of dignity and self-respect, Jane.

Doing what's right because you require it of yourself as a person should always be part of any questionable situation or tough dating decision. *Right* for you is equally as important as right by societal standards. In other words, if you and Dick have been dating for four weeks and you just don't feel like dating other people anymore, you don't need to wonder whether or not he still is. Choosing to behave in a certain way while involved with someone is as much your decision alone as it is a joint one when the topic comes up.

No, you can't expect him to do the same or punish him for not feeling equally as strong or following suit quickly enough for your tastes. You need him to respect his own feelings, but this should not prevent you from respecting yours too and acting upon them. Being fair makes the practice of dating easier to manage because it helps to bring clarity where needed.

In certain cases, however, how you feel and what you do about a particular Dick becomes rather obvious quickly, especially when the two of you are laughing together all the time, whether over a fumbled word met by a clever retort that set you two rolling or while attending a comedic performance enhanced by a great dinner and a ton of hand-holding and wet kisses. Being compatible, whatever the circumstances you encounter, not only makes dating fun and easy but will make the potential for long term relationship success more real.

All things being equal, I recommend you stick with the Dick who tickles your fancy as easily as possible. You are sure to have a lot of laughs regardless of what others think or how routine your life, together, may become.

CHAPTER 42

JANE BREAKS UP WITH DICK

If you do decide that the Dick you are dating is just not for you, the manner in which you break up with him needs to correlate with how many times you've actually seen him. We live in a world that offers all types of communication to do the dirty deed. That said, however, don't break up with a guy over text unless you've dated him only briefly. Anything more than that is just not right. Again, be fair when contemplating how to break up with a Dick who probably really likes you and wants to get to know you more.

A quick but sensitive phone call will rarely land you on Dick's Facebook timeline with the phrase, "What a bitch!" next to your photo and a huge warning sign positioned above both. Dating for a month or so requires a face-to-face meeting coupled with a reasonable explanation, in my opinion. Although this approach is the least comfortable of all of the options, it is the right and respectful thing to do for both of you. It will allow you to potentially go on as friends or at least won't brand you a "coward" and not date-worthy by another guy who happens to fancy you and knows him.

Think long term, Jane, when ousting any Dick, now and in the future. You won't believe how unbelievably small this world actually is until the day you run into the Dick you carelessly dumped in college walking behind you at a job interview with a company owned by his pop...or by him for that matter. It always happens when the stakes are highest and you least expect it. I kid you not.

Such incidents can easily be avoided if you put yourself in the shoes of the Dick you are no longer interested in spending time with and act accordingly. No doubt, dating provides you a great deal of opportunity to become good at this.

The entire process is one giant learning experience made up of lots of tiny learning experiences that can, at times, make you feel as if you are completely incompetent, especially in the beginning when it feels as if you are venturing forth blindly.

No doubt, the Dicks you choose today will be different from the Dicks you choose tomorrow or those you chose yesterday. As we evolve, so do our dating tastes and needs. That said, however, there are some Janes who just never adjust their wish lists appropriately, even though their lives (for all intent and purposes) reflect stability and growth. You know the gal. She's 35 and still dating the Dick with the great buns but nothing else worth her attention. Their dating relationship lasts for about two minutes, and then the next guy with another set of great buns comes along. Unfortunately, this Jane wants to get married but has no idea how to commence down the road. It's a common insanity that women have difficulty breaking from.

The answer, however, is incredibly simple and here it is: *Do something different*! In other words, change your norm and accompany a guy whom you would not usually accept an invitation from, then consider sticking with him for a while. Yes, it will be uncomfortable in the beginning, but so is the ending of every relationship that hasn't worked out. And at least, there is hope alive here.

Sometimes, we Janes need to accept that we are our own worst enemy when it comes to getting what we really want. We overcomplicate matters, using every excuse except the one living inside of us that is screaming how wrong our internal programming is specific to finding a Dick who would actually make a great long-term partner. I had this issue myself and realized it two years after my graduation from college. Prior to that moment, I had been choosing the type of guy I thought I wanted but not the type of guy I actually needed. When I finally became fed up enough with every one of my relationships being unfulfilling or not working out, I decided that the hardwiring responsible for my dating choices sucked. I needed to do something different to counteract my initial instincts. So I did.

Eventually, I would accept a date with a gentleman that I probably would not have given the time of day prior to my making the conscious decision to change my behavior. We married shortly after that and went on to have four beautiful children, a great big house, lots of love, and an amazing life together. We shared "the fairy tale" until the day he died. When I think back as to how I might never have known him had I remained stuck in my old ways, I can't even imagine it.

This is the reason I am advising you. If what you're doing isn't working, change it. Only through **discomfort** and **decision** do true personal and dating growth develop. You need to push past your norm, pull close the Dick who might not fit the mold you've become accustomed to, and hang on tight. He will open you up to possibilities that you may not know otherwise. At a minimum, he will expand your tastes in ways that will eventually help you to find **the one** if he ultimately is not it.

The only person who can prevent you from dating the guy who treats you the way you want to be treated and lands you where you want to go is you. You are never stuck unless you force yourself to be. If one type of Dick isn't working for you, find another type and expect the internal stretching that will occur along the way to challenge the very reason you are putting yourself through the pain.

Once you climb over that hump, you will be grateful that you did. I know I am. A single decision changed my entire life for the better. Imagine whom you could meet if you made your own?

<u>Love</u>

A love that's easily defined
fools the heart and numbs the mind.
A love that sets itself apart
boggles the mind and stirs the heart.

CHAPTER 43

JANE NEEDS DICK

Men are not wallets. Neither are women, for that matter, but men are more apt to be perceived as one when dating, simply because of the way our society has functioned up to now. Plus, men tend to bring home the majority share of the bacon still.

That said, to choose a man without being able to stand on your own two feet *financially*, Jane, hinders your ability to choose your Dick wisely. Don't be surprised if you come up short in the love department if you shortchange yourself in the prep work required to make a good decision.

The more empowered you feel in your own right, the more freedom you will afford yourself in choosing a proper Dick. That alone should compel you to do the necessary work to set yourself up for success from the get go, as this is your life, Jane, and it can be a tragically long one if you choose a Dick purely on the basis of financial security. This doesn't mean that he shouldn't be able to carry his own weight or possess viable ambition. It means you need to count other characteristics of his before you count his pennies.

On the flip side, there is an emptiness in being loved solely for what you can produce. Men have experienced this for years, and more and more women lately are feeling it too, as Jane begins to outearn Dick due to the changing economic times and employment landscape. Even so, this is a reality that is hard to stomach no matter which gender you are.

This isn't to say that men resent being the primary breadwinners in their homes if they believe that they are loved and respected for it. It just means that without that, it's a hollow victory for them, and that's where the problems begin.

When you don't need a man for his money but you need him because you can't bear the idea of being without him simply because you love him (and like him) that much, you are in a very good position to choose the right Dick. You are also in a very good position to set the rules of the relationship, dating and otherwise, in a way that truly suits you and makes him happy too. You are foolish, Jane, to do this any other way. The more solid and steady you are, the more confident your Dick will be in you and your future together. Once he gets past the idea that you don't need him for his money—something that boggles the minds of many men initially—he will come to quite like the realities of being needed for himself. It is a notion that many men never thought they'd have the luxury of considering.

At the same time, Jane, you've fallen off your rocking horse if you think that you don't have to continue to secure his ego by making sure your Dick knows that you do *need* him. Men need to be needed, and if you fail at this with him, don't be surprised if he fails you, which is the reason I noted earlier the importance of filling his head with legitimate compliments and recognizing the big and little contributions he makes to your life. His identity depends on it. If a guy doesn't know who he is in your eyes, he loses himself, which may just lead him to look outward for confirmation and a purpose.

Wandering Dicks don't do well on their own. They usually screw a lot of things up, including your life, when in a confused frame of mind. In order to avoid this, make sure you do your part by making him feel needed and telling him regularly.

The more you do this, the more likely he is to show you why the best decision you ever made was to begin dating him. If not, your Dick needs help, and much more than you can ever give him. Rush him to a good psychiatrist for an examination and a chat. The man has the best of both worlds at his feet. His love and admiration for you should be swelling as opposed to shrinking in size...like every other part of him.

And take heart, Jane; you walked into this relationship with two strong limbs underneath you. Either plant them firmly on the ground till this Dick figures out which direction is up, or let them carry you out for good. You've got the rest of your life to live, and those stellar tootsies of yours will find another, more befitting bedfellow to rub up against. Be thankful you have them and walk on forward. With every step you take, you will be one step closer to meeting the perfect Dick for you. That's how dating works, Jane, I assure you. So stay focused, keep moving, and never look back. And remember, just as you are looking for him, he's out there looking for you too.

CHAPTER 44

DICK AND JANE DANCE

It befuddles me why women would ever want to spend time with Dicks who don't truly want them. It can't make them feel good about themselves or special in any way. And it is a hell of a lot of work, constantly substantiating the worthiness of someone's affection. That dynamic is really self-destructive, Jane, and will never launch a relationship between the two of you off the ground. The only catalyst that can do this is the one that underscores his craziness for you, which is met equally by your own for him.

Your dating experience is vastly different when you spend time with a Dick who can't get you out of his mind versus one who can, and does, the moment he drops you back off at your humble abode...or crawls from your bed in the middle of the night and leaves you wondering what happened to him. That's a shitty feeling to be left with and a dramatically different one than you will experience with a guy who actually wants to take you to the dance, stay through to the next morning, and make coffee while he lets you sleep a little longer. That's the guy you should give a true shot to, Jane. Not the loser who has nothing to offer you but a momentary high, followed by a catastrophic low.

Always go to the dance with the guy who wants to take you and leave with him too. You will know that Dick because he's the man who continues to make it perfectly clear how much he likes you. He'd literally live on your doorstep, if he needed to, just to win you over and it wasn't creepy. He will be the one to care for you and take care of you, even when you are perfectly capable of doing so yourself. The Dick who will hold your hair back when death is undeniably staring you in the face from the toilet bowl. The guy who will gallantly wrap you in his jacket even when you insist you don't need it despite the obvious chicken skin spreading across your arms and legs. If you haven't figured it out yet, those are all telltale signs that this man wants you, and he's making sure you know it.

Don't confuse his focus, attention or concern for you with his being a pushover, inspiring you to precariously and easily write him off. Many women do this, only to eventually look back with regret as they, once again, park themselves on the couch with a pint of mint chocolate chip ice cream and that cat previously mentioned, the one that they picked up at the animal rescue center earlier and now call Gary.

Be grateful that this Dick showed up and take the time to get to know him. Even if the attraction is not mutual at first, it might develop over time. This happens to many Janes, women who have grown tired of all the disappointing dates and games. By the way, that's not *settling*. That's maturing and seeing dating (and life) through wiser, more experienced eyes.

Love happens every which way, and sometimes the most powerful love arises when you least expect it and out of circumstances you could never have predicted. It is a dance between the heart, mind, and two people who decide to go along together and then decided to *stay together* on the eternal playdate. But before you actually find it, you need to accept the invitation from the guy who really wants to take you, not the guy who really wants to leave you, Jane. You'd do better spending another night in the company of Gary, whose cattin' around won't hurt you nearly as much.

CONCLUSION

So, Jane, as we have now reached the end of my dating advice for the moment, think about all that I have shared when the next Dick approaches you with something to say. If he wants you, you will know it. No guesswork; no translation; no reinterpretation required.

If you have to query a friend to figure out what his words or actions mean when he is standing right next to you, they mean that he isn't interested. You won't need to *query* if he is interested, as he will remove all confusion from the play. It will then be up to you to decide whether or not you want to catch his ball.

As you seem to have handicapped your dating life, love life, and romantic future enough already—otherwise why read this book—try answering him while abiding by the wisdom I've provided. You might just see an upswing in your dating results. And if, by chance, you happen to end up moving from dating to living *happily ever after* with this Dick, send an invitation my way or find me on social media and let me know. I will be overjoyed to hear the good news and learn that I've helped.

For everyone else, I leave you with this. Dating is as elementary today as it has ever been. The basics have not changed, and neither has Dick. Those are the ABCs of it, Jane, and you can either accept them and help yourself or not. If you do, the only thing that you have to lose is your own loneliness and, quite possibly, the few drawers in your bedroom that have been patiently awaiting the right Dick to come along and fill them.

ABOUT THE AUTHOR

Laura J. Wellington is the CEO and Founder of THREADMB.com. She is an influencer, entrepreneur, author, and an award-winning television creator, including four Tellys and The Forbes Enterprise Award. Widowed at a young age, Laura is mom to five kids.